THE
GRAND
GUIGNOL

THEATRE OF FEAR AND TERROR

Revised Edition

MEL GORDON

DA CAPO PRESS
NEW YORK

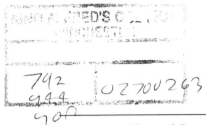
Library of Congress Cataloging-in-Publication Data

The Grand Guignol: theatre of fear and terror / [edited by] Mel Gordon.
   p.   cm.
   Originally published: New York: Amok Press, 1988.
   Includes bibliographical references.
   ISBN 0-306-80806-4 (alk. paper)
   1. Théâtre du Grand-Guignol—History. I. Gordon, Mel.
PN2636.P4G75   1997
792′.0944′36—dc21   97-17646
                                                 CIP

Book Design by Beth Escott

ACKNOWLEDGEMENTS

Like the Grand Guignol itself, this book is the product of many artistic talents. Chief among these are Ken Swezey, Beth Escott, the book's original designer and art director, Don Kennison and Mary Granfield for editorial assistance, and J.T. Steiny for his illustrations. Also deserving meaty recognition for their unstinting support are Christophe Bourseiller, Sean Burke, Jeff Casper, André Gisiger, Daniel Gerould, Shade Rupe, and Yuval Taylor.

First Da Capo Press edition 1997

This Da Capo Press paperback edition of *The Grand Guignol* is a revised republication of the edition published in New York in 1988. The changes and additions are as follows: a new foreword, minor textual emendations, the substitution of the play *A Crime in a Madhouse* for *The Laboratory of Hallucinations*, and numerous substitutions of images. It is published by arrangement with the author.

Translation of André de Lorde's *The System of Dr. Goudron and Prof. Plume* © 1988 Jeff Casper and Amok Press. Translation of André de Lorde and Alfred Binet's *A Crime in a Madhouse* copyright © 1997 by André Gisiger and Mel Gordon.

Original art by J.T. Steiny. All other art is from original Grand Guignol sources, which include program art, publicity stills, and posters. We have contacted copyright owners where known.

Published by Da Capo Press, Inc.
A Subsidiary of Plenum Publishing Corporation
233 Spring Street, New York, N.Y. 10013

To Hal Prince,
the newest "bandit"
of the Grand Guignol.

FOREWORD TO THE REVISED EDITION

DRUNKEN AND RAMPAGING NATIVE militia discover an isolated lunatic asylum in a jungle clearing in Central Africa. They lock the doors and toss dozens of grenades through the windows. The mental patients begin to sing and dance hysterically, not knowing the charge and shrapnel from the grenades are meant to kill them. Two brothers, almost identically dressed, quietly sneak into the den of their upper-middle-class house and methodically gun down their parents, who themselves are transfixed by a television soap opera. Caught in a web of an absolute panic, three black middle-aged sisters, fearing Satan's power unleashed in a hoodoo parish of Louisiana, flee to a small town in Texas, where they stop to gouge out the eyes of their possessed but acquiescent younger sister. A suicide cult, led by a castrated prophet, spends its last days on earth gleefully playing nickel slot machines in a Las Vegas casino, riding roller coasters, and searching for lost coins in an amusement park. Believing that his former wife has given him a deadly blood disease, a celebrity athlete cuts her throat in the middle of the night and repeatedly stabs an innocent admirer of hers. Although his blood is found everywhere at the crime scene, he is acquitted and lives out his days, playing golf and reconsidering his career options.

The Grand Guignol, the unimaginably gory theatre of terror and horror that addicted countless generations of Parisian theatre-goers and thrill-seeking tourists, never died. Its cruelties and perverse comedy seep into our daily lives. Unlike the Gothic melodramas of the nineteenth century, the Grand Guignol—from its inception in 1897 to its humiliating death in 1962—based its plots on bloody and murderous criminal exploits, which were taken from real life. The newspaper, the laboratory report, the prefect's roster—those were the sources of the Guignol's unpredictable and grisly productions. Audiences also sensed that this was a different kind of entertainment. When bones crunched and blood started to coagulate on the performer's matted hair, the aesthetic cessation of disbelief began. But this was quickly supported by the spectator's deepest understanding that the shocking stage display was a more truthful unveiling of the savage human soul than anything available on stage or in the cinema. Only life matched the horror of the Grand Guignol.

The folklore of the Theatre of the Grand Guignol is virtually endless. A few additional facts and surprises: during the last, confused years of World War One, horribly wounded French soldiers were trucked into Paris for a day, where they were wined and dined in fine restaurants and in the evening brought to watch the Grand Guignol as a special treat. Internal French military files after the war reported that this worked as a great morale builder.

Alfred Binet, the French creator of the Binet Intelligence Test, was one of the most successful playwrights of the Grand Guignol and co-author of *A Crime in a Madhouse*. The American Psychological Society in the early twenties agonized over Binet's original examination, which asked such thought-provoking questions to young students as: "What is the first thing that you would do, if you came home after school and found your mother strangled and mutilated?" Nearly all of Binet's horrific essay tests were deleted in the American versions.

In the post–World War Two era, all three owners and many of the directors of the Grand Guignol were women, including one of France's leading feminist intellectuals. Despite the Grand Guignol's disturbing reputation for graphic onstage mayhem against defenseless young waifs, it stood out as one of the few French institutions that gave full creative reign to female producers. But women-directed or not, the Grand Guignol quickly floundered commercially in its final incarnations.

Neither establishment theatre nor *outré* art, the Grand Guignol inhabited a marshy no-man's land of authentic, if historically expiring, popular entertainment in the fifties. The overall devotion among Parisian writers, society people, and artists to the Grand Guignol at the time is surprisingly difficult to assess. Many continued to attend its performances with fascinating regularity but without comment. Probably, like the assemblages of pornographic photographs sealed in wafer-thin wraps— Montmartre's backstreet specialty—the Grand Guignol was insufficiently primitive, ironic, or even esoteric enough to overtly influence their avant-garde sensibilities. The trip to 20bis Rue Chaptal apparently degenerated in that decade into an anthropological search for lost and curious theatre pleasures.

But the dying Grand Guignol had another legacy. Its bitter idealism, distrust of authority, and reckless sexual taunting was certainly passed on to a postwar generation of European artists—although in ways that are still too murky, too disguised and subterranean to be easily traced. Writing in her diary in the spring of 1958, Anaïs Nin typically bemoaned the Grand Guignol's current decline, yet she also revealed its deepest, truest, and most invisible impact on its knowing spectators: "I surrendered myself to the Grand Guignol, to its venerable filth which used to cause such shivers of horror, which used to petrify us with terror. All our nightmares of sadism and perversion were played out on that stage."

TABLE OF CONTENTS

"The most sick, perverted, and pornographic drama on Broadway can never hope to match the thrillers staged at the Grand Guignol."
—RAGE *(a sensationalist New York magazine)*
March 1963

"Tragic pleasure consists in the imitation of horrifying and pitiful events which in itself, according to Aristotle, is delightful."
—Compendium of Tragicomic Poetry
by Giovanni Battista Guarini
1599

THE GRAND GUIGNOL:
THEATRE OF FEAR AND TERROR

HERE IS SOMETHING EMBARRASSING about the Grand Guignol. Like a renegade sect or invented religion from another century, it still touches upon our secret longings and fears. A product of *fin-de-siècle* France, the Grand Guignol managed to transgress theatrical conventions and outrage its public as it explored the back alleys of unfettered desire, aesthetic impropriety, and nascent psychological trends in criminology and the study of abnormal behavior. Its supporters called the Grand Guignol play the most Aristotelian of twentieth-century dramatic forms since it was passionately devoted to the purgation of fear and pity. Audiences came to the Theatre of the Grand Guignol to be frightened, to be shocked, while simultaneously delighting in their fears (or in those of the people around them). The more terrifying a performance was—that is, the more it tapped into the collective phobias of its spectators—the greater the success it achieved.

If one had to single out one reason for the Grand Guignol's 65 years of prosperity and success from 1897 to 1962 (although it certainly had its share of ups and downs), no doubt a special genius for finding new audiences in every generation would have to be considered. In some decades, the Parisian Theatre of Fear and Terror was the darling of Paris' *épater les bourgeois* intelligentsia and their followers; in other times, its elite spectators consisted of an odd mix of cocaine-sniffing royal outcasts from a dozen lost Central European and Balkan Houses and thrill-seeking tourists. More often than not, seats were taken by regulars, a special class of spectator, the "Guignolers." But no matter when the Grand Guignol actors performed or who watched, it played a topsy-turvy game with its audience's deepest instincts and underlying, repressed impulses for sex and savage retribution.

That studies of the Grand Guignol have been largely ignored in scholarly circles should come as no surprise. Here was a theatre genre that was predicated on the stimulation of the rawest and most adolescent of human interactions and desires: incest and patricide; blood lust; sexual anxiety and conflict; morbid fascination with bodily mutilation and death; loathing of authority; fear of insanity; an overall disgust for the human condition and its imperfect institutions. For the vast majority of drama academicians, however, the Grand Guignol was little more than an unhealthy curiosity, unworthy of serious analysis or documentation. Despite its immense popularity and influence on other dramatic forms in the twenties and thirties, such as the Hollywood horror film and psychological thriller, no major theatre history text, even today, as much as mentions Paris' greatest twentieth-century stage attraction.

Part of the problem certainly lies with an intrinsic humor embedded in the Grand Guignol's plots and techniques. Unfortunately, journalists and critics made little distinction between the black and antinomian humor of violent fantasy, especially as it was played out in minute detail on the Grand Guignol stage, and the self-conscious, melodramatic enactments of camp parody. When tyrannical fathers are surgically mutilated, when innocent children are strangled in their beds, when mothers leave their infants to starve on their neighbors' doorsteps, when all the familiar taboos of social constraint and sex are challenged and then overturned in the most graphic manner imaginable, at first, laughter and derision seem to be the appropriate responses from the normal spectator. But in a typical Grand Guignol evening, laughter was always followed by panic and, after that, by more laughter still. Laughter was the dark and hidden ingredient of the Grand Guignol.

A HISTORY OF THE GRAND GUIGNOL

N A WAY, THE GRAND GUIGNOL always existed. The impulse to shock, to display the extremes of human behavior, and then to demonstrate the divine punishments that follow for those individuals who violate society's taboos may have been the original social function of all performance. This attempt to force from theatre a seriousness— a playing with life and death—could take place within or outside the pale of official taste, which was later labeled "high" or "low" art. In the preliterate world, shamanistic enactments of self-mutilation brought fascinated tribespeople into new and altered states of awareness. Human, animal, and effigy sacrifices were the centerpieces of civilization's earliest ceremonies in Egypt and the New World.

Normally in Western cultures, horrific events on stage were permitted as long as they were obvious imitations. Yet Aeschylus so frightened his Greek audience during *The Eumenides* that "children died and pregnant women miscarried." Promptbooks from the Middle Ages reveal an awful and bloody display of animal parts that realistically substituted for performers' severed limbs and organs. The early Elizabethan and Jacobean playwrights (Shakespeare excelling among them) feverishly constructed plots and dialogues that remain among the most unwholesome and disturbing in the world repertoire. (Artaud even included Shakespeare, Dekker, and Webster as charter playwrights in his Theatre of Cruelty.)

Pornographic dramatic entertainments were played out in the brothels of seventeenth and eighteenth-century Vienna and Paris while court poets dourly spelled out Neoclassical rules of writing and acting to playwrights and censoring boards. Around the Place de la Nation during the French Revolution's Reign of Terror, freshly-guillotined corpses were manipulated like oversized puppets in grotesque comedies. Throughout the eighteenth and nineteenth centuries, as the European theatre lost its royal patronage and audience as well as its artistic efficacy, other strange "blood-and-guts" performances were mounted in conjunction with the revival of occultism and Mesmerism. Once again, violence and sexuality reigned in these private rituals and "scientific" presentations, darkly conducted by shrewd director-prophets who reenacted milder but more sophisticated renditions of shamanistic trickery.

Felicien Rops. *La Peine de Mort*

LE PETIT CRUCIFIÉ

ROMANCE
Créée par MARIUS RICHARD, à la Scala

Paroles de   Petit format, 0 fr. 35   Musique de

René ESSE ✳ Gaston MAQUIS

HENRI PASCAL, éditeur, 38, rue Tiquetonne, PARIS

Successeur d'Albert REPOS

"The fait divers *prefigured on the printed page what the Grand Guignol would be on the stage."*

As the Industrial Revolution intensified during the first quarter of the nineteenth century, a thirst for new and lurid popular entertainment forms grew in Western Europe. Most of these traded on sensationalistic plots and the exploitation of their audiences' visceral curiosity over morbid criminal behavior and savage punishment. In a way, they acted as fantasy substitutes for the guillotine and its public celebrations. Guilbert de Pixérécourt, an unhappy graduate of the Counterrevolutionary and Republican armies, created an ironclad recipe for the newest subliterary genre called the melodrama. In his plays, everything began with the complete and unexpected victimization of poor and innocent people by a cruel and sexually corrupt oppressor, quickly followed by a superhuman struggle that always concluded with a swift—almost divine—punishment against the agents of human iniquity. By the 1810s, as many as seventy melodramatic productions a month opened on Paris' underclass thoroughfare, the Boulevard du Crime. Each play seemed to release a previously hidden psychic spring among the working-class people from Glasgow to Dresden, with its dramatic hub in industrial Paris.

But if the early melodrama gave crude organization to the feverish desires and imaginations of young proletarian Europeans, another popular artistic genre spoke more authoritatively still to the heart and head of those looking for grisly amusements. This was the *faits divers*, or the short news items printed in broadsheets or yellow journals. From the time of the French Revolution to the 1930s, specialized French newspapers and weeklys provided their readers with realistic and gory accounts of true-life crime stories and their frequently bizarre denouements. While the *fait divers* covered much of the same plot and character terrain of the gothic and cheap melodrama—abandoned infants, seduction and rape, public assassinations, forced prostitution, freaks of nature, suicides, sadistic abuse by the powerful, incest, drownings and suffocations, spiritualism, train wrecks, child abuse, mutilation, and other crimes of passion—they differed from de Pixérécourt's invention in three aspects. For one, the *faits divers*, as befitting their name, were short in length. Usually illustrated with garishly-colored drawings, they rarely needed to hold the reader's attention for more than a few minutes. Secondly, unlike the melodramas, which had to end happily, the *fait divers* normally concluded with a disturbing and vindictive note. Finally, the *fait divers'* plots were taken from life, not from the pens of fantasy-mad playwrights. In these ways, the *fait divers* prefigured exactly on the printed page what the Grand Guignol would be on the stage.

The School of Naturalism

The Theatre of the Grand Guignol was one of several offshoots from the Naturalist movement on the Parisian stage that began in the late 1880s. The Théâtre Libre, founded by a twenty-nine year-old gas company clerk, Andre Antoine, heeded Emile Zola's call that the theatre must become naturalist or nothing at all. Yet between Zola's manifesto for a "scientific" theatre, based on a methodical analysis of human behavior, heredity, and environment

LA PHOTOGRAPHIE DANS LES PRISONS.

"Theatre Libre's short plays dealt with the mess and squalor of lowlife among Paris' underclasses."

in 1873, and Antoine's stripped-down stage experiments, some fourteen years had elapsed. By 1887, naturalism and its accompanying radical philosophies no longer offended free-thinking Parisians.

The Théâtre Libre (a wishful name, since it was paid for out of Antoine's dwindling resources) made its renown for other reasons. Actual used furniture, replete with nicks and stains, and objects from daily life, such as sides of beef and clucking chickens, were brought to the stage. Interestingly, some of these were hastily purchased from a derelict, second-hand furniture store when less dilapidated articles borrowed from Antoine's mother's apartment were stolen just before the Théâtre Libre's opening night. Antoine also pioneered an innovative acting style that more or less ignored its audience. His spectators were startled to find the Théâtre Libre actors speaking to one another with their backs to the house as if the audience was secretly observing through an invisible wall. (A contemporary circus parody of Antoine showed a clown with two backs of a head instead of a face.) More appalling still, many of the Théâtre Libre's short plays dealt with the mess and squalor of lowlife among Paris' underclasses.

From the inauguration of the Théâtre Libre's brave experiment in naturalist dramaturgy, Antoine demonstrated an artistic generosity and eclecticism uncharacteristic of the time. Since naturalistic dramas tended to be diminutive in length, as many as five or six one-acts might comprise a single evening at Antoine's 373-seat theatre. But there were never enough talented naturalist playwrights to satisfy Antoine's needs. So besides naturalist plays, verse tragedies, adaptations from classic

Felicien Rops. *La Buveuse d'absinthe*

literature, comedies, even proto-Symbolist sketches appeared during the Théâtre Libre's five-year heyday. And as the Théâtre Libre's repertoire began to move toward the ethereal and ineffable mindscape of the burgeoning Symbolist movement, there was a corresponding pull toward extreme naturalism, or what would soon be called "sordid realism." These sensational and offensive plays, which often brought high-minded critics into civic and censorious action against them, fell into at least two separate camps: the dark, anti-clerical mystery fable and the grisly social documentary of modern Paris.

Typical of the handful of naturalist mystery plays was Auguste Linert's *A Christmas Story* (1890). Like a host of young French writers of his generation, Linert became fascinated with Edgar Allan Poe's hideous and irony-laced short stories, somewhat amplified in Baudelaire's colorful translations. In Linert's *A Christmas Story*, a familiar tale unfolded with a shocking conclusion: on Christmas eve, a peasant-girl, in her last term of pregnancy, looks for a place to give birth. Unable to find some kindly soul who will take her in, she murders her infant child and throws the remains to a farmer's pigs, while in the distance, neighboring peasants sing Christmas carols on their way to Midnight Mass.

No less disturbing were the Théâtre Libre's documentary plays that recreated slices of life from Paris' underworld. Called

rosse, or "crass," plays (from the street argot for a nasty or malicious person; literally "old horse"), these productions revealed a different, more primitive thought process, a universe of pure animal passion. Thievery, prostitution, alcohol addiction, sexual dependence and humiliation, jealousy, incest, child abuse, cheating, brutality to women, and vengeance were the most common and notorious themes. And if the characters lived in an atmosphere devoid of bourgeois mores and guilt, the plays themselves shattered the middle-class expectations of Antoine's spectators. All the bourgeois concepts of love and loyalty followed a new and skewed logic. Wrong-doers (that is, the criminals, sociopaths, and young hooligans: the *apaches*) were rarely punished or praised. Almost always, *apache* life with its anti-social, indigenous traditions and conventions continued unabated at the play's end.

In addition to their novel subject matter, the *rosse* productions created havoc with the aesthetic and ironclad structural components of the well-made play. Here, none of the normative values of French society—good and evil, simple "right and wrong," the hierarchy of one class over another— existed. Nothing *had* to happen in a *rosse* play. Any conclusion was possible. Naturally, these amoral and unsettling naturalistic dramas proved to annoy the pundits of establishment mores even more than Antoine's tattered sofas and realistic acting. The Théâtre Libre was under immense pressure to rid itself of both the naturalist mystery play and social documentary. Only because the Théâtre Libre ran itself as a private enterprise limited to individual subscribers were local censors held at bay.

"Rosse *plays revealed a different,*
more primitive thought process,
a universe of pure animal passion."

*"Méténier brought Antoine to a
private viewing of the police execution
of a criminal."*

Oscar Méténier

Formerly a secretary to the Police Commissioner of Paris and a writer for tabloid-like journals, Oscar Méténier was considered the master of the *rosse* play along with naturalist playwrights George Ancey and Jean Jullien. A co-founder of the Théâtre Libre in 1887, the twenty-eight year-old Méténier provided Antoine with many of his most controversial offerings. Having already scoured Paris' menacing red-light and working-class slum districts for over six years in a scientific search for naturalist material, Méténier brought an immediate and striking authenticity of character, atmosphere, and language into his writings and dramas. He also exhibited a genuine sympathy for his lowlife play figures, many of whom were based on real persons, and he found their instinctive and savage actions superior to the vain pretensions of Paris' bourgeois theatre-goers.

Méténier's *rosse* vignettes were brief, rarely longer than fifteen minutes, but lurid and effective. *In the Family*, the sensation of the Théâtre Libre's second evening, mounted on May 30th, 1887, glimpsed into the lives of the Parisian underclass. In an illicit shop for the purchase of stolen merchandise, a thoroughly alcoholic thug; his daughter, a streetwalker; and a son, who pimps for a living, meet for dinner. The son describes the public execution of his best friend by guillotine that day in crude, stinging detail. Preoccupied and untouched by the young man's story, the father and sister finish dinner and ready themselves for their nocturnal and illegal activities. *In the Family* was quickly labeled an affront to public morality and banned from production in public theatres. In 1889, *The Informer* (*La Casserole*), Méténier's more full-length play,

lasting some thirty minutes, again shocked and titillated the Théâtre Libre critics. Using real criminal types to play themselves in minor parts and an actual circus strongman, the violent sketch unfolded in a cheap dance hall, recreated in naturalistic detail. There, in a bloody climax, a pimp grows enraged at a prostitute who has informed on his male lover and stabs her to death.

Méténier continued to work for the Théâtre Libre, once adapting Leo Tolstoy's *Power of Darkness* in a Parisian street argot that gained the approval of the Russian master himself. Another time, Méténier suggested that his untrained brother be cast for a part in a *rosse* play. But Antoine grew tired of the offensive and vulgar genre. In its unpredictability, it was predictable. To Antoine, the difference between a great *rosse* play and a hackneyed one seemed slight. And when Méténier brought Antoine to a private viewing of a criminal's execution, the director of the Théâtre Libre found much less enjoyment in the spectacle than the chronicler of *apache* life. Méténier and Antoine were moving in different directions.

Then, in 1893, six years after its beginnings, Antoine's Théâtre Libre disappeared from its Montmartre home. It had collapsed financially. Yet naturalism in the theatre had not spent its force. In just a few years, it would succeed wildly beyond anyone's prediction, except perhaps Zola's. The novelty of realistic sets and a more life-like style of acting invigorated the Parisian scene in the middle and late 1890s. The plots, though, would change, once again centering on the foibles and etiquette of middle class life. The shocking jargon of the streets that Méténier made stageworthy would now fuel the witty and slightly suggestive lyrics of the popular cabaret chansons.

"He called it the Grand Guignol after the name of the popular Punch and Judy puppet character."

The Founding of the Grand Guignol

In the spring of 1897, Méténier, who had now tried his hand at other literary pursuits, including the writing of vaudevilles, returned to his patented *rosse* genre. He opened the Theatre of the Grand Guignol at 20 rue Chaptal, not far from the original Théâtre Libre. In fact, his 285-seat theatre (variously given as 280, 272, 265 and 230 seats) seemed like a grisly extension of the Théâtre Libre. It was said that he called it the Grand Guignol after the name of "Guignol," the popular Punch and Judy puppet character from Lyons, which had become a generic name for all puppet entertainments. It was

to be a "Grand" (large) "Guignol" (puppet show) since the intended audiences were to be adults and the characters live performers. The mad behavior and violence that excite children in a normal guignol would be magnified for the pleasure of their parents. ("Grand Guignol" might have been borrowed from a contemporary satirical review of the same name.)

The actual space of the Theatre of the Grand Guignol had a curious and celebrated history. Erected as a Jansenist refuge and convent in 1786, it was gutted and sacked five years later during the Reign of Terror. In the early nineteenth century, a blacksmith with an artistic bent refurbished the chapel's remains as his workshop, leaving untouched the wooden angels hanging from the paneled ceilings in the foyer, and the pseudo-gothic designs cut into the thick oak doors. Throughout the 1870s, the conservative, fire-and-brimstone Dominican priest, Father Didon, used the back-alley Montmartre church as a pulpit to attack the purveyors of extramarital sex. Then in 1880, Georges Rochgrosse, a leading academic painter and designer, purchased the old baroque chapel for use as his studio.

Finally, Maurice Magnier, a fanatical publisher with a shaky financial past, leased it in 1896, with the hope that he could ride the trend, inspired by Antoine, for intimate performances given in Montmartre chamber theatres. Calling his venture the Théâtre-Salon, Magnier planned to mount a series of miniature dramas and one-act plays. But little went right. The forbidding, twenty-by-twenty foot stage seemed too small even for a cabaret theatre. One critic joked that it was so cramped inside that a front-row spectator could shake hands with the actors

*"Maurey sought sure-fire
formulas of terror and fear."*

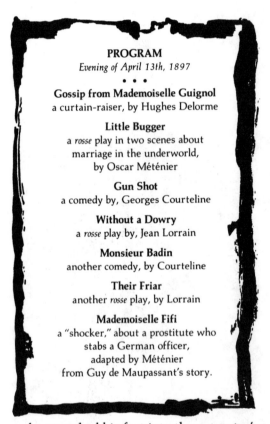

PROGRAM
Evening of April 13th, 1897

• • •

Gossip from Mademoiselle Guignol
a curtain-raiser, by Hughes Delorme

Little Bugger
a *rosse* play in two scenes about
marriage in the underworld,
by Oscar Méténier

Gun Shot
a comedy by, Georges Courteline

Without a Dowry
a *rosse* play by, Jean Lorrain

Monsieur Badin
another comedy, by Courteline

Their Friar
another *rosse* play, by Lorrain

Mademoiselle Fifi
a "shocker," about a prostitute who
stabs a German officer,
adapted by Méténier
from Guy de Maupassant's story.

mocked and wrongly used, appealed to his sense of the gothic. (Decades later, "Guignolers" would swear that they heard the actual whispers and chants of nuns during frenzied and agonizing segments of the horror plays.) Also, the claustrophobic confinement of the house could greatly improve the acoustics and, therefore, the nastiness of the *rosse* plays.

With a good deal of fanfare, Méténier inaugurated his Theatre of the Grand Guignol on April 13th, 1897. Dressed in black, as always, and accompanied by two body guards, as always, Méténier triumphantly walked down the orchestra aisle, shouting and accepting greetings in his bullfrog voice. The first program consisted of seven plays: a curtain raiser, two *rosse* plays by Méténier, two comedies by Georges Courteline, and two dramas by Jean Lorrain. The evening was unusual enough to be considered a success, even in a jaded Paris.

Méténier wanted the repertoire of the Grand Guignol to be different from the disbanded Théâtre Libre and the Théâtre-Salon. Short comedies would alternate with *rosse* plays. Each would intensify the other, like "hot and cold showers." After the first season, a typical bill of Méténier's Grand Guignol would consist of 1) a slapstick curtain raiser, 2) a light drama, 3) a comedy, 4) the horror play, and 5) a farce. Much like a vaudeville format, these plays could be replaced or repeated at will from week to week. *Mademoiselle Fifi* played continuously on one bill or another for seven months. The determining factor was the play's immediate and overall structural effectiveness on its audience. Méténier's formula of "hot and cold showers" was unwittingly responsible for saving the Continental one-

as he stretched his feet into the prompter's box. Literally, any audience member who arose from his pew-like seat during a performance unintentionally became a part of the show. Magnier failed again.

Oscar Méténier had different ideas about the old chapel. Like the blacksmith-artist before him, he retained the stiff and heavy architectural artifacts from the *ancien regime* period. He especially adored the wicked-looking cherubs with their crooked smiles that were carved into the beams of the vaulted ceilings, and the shallow church-like seats in the balcony. The anxious and cursed atmosphere of a huge confessional booth, act play from extinction.

To accommodate the Grand Guignol repertoire, Méténier further divided his *rosse* plays into two categories: 1) Plays of Popular Manners, virtually actionless dramas of Parisian lowlife that indirectly ridiculed bourgeois morality and propriety, such as *In the Family* and *Little Bugger*; and 2) Newspaper Items (the *faits divers*), dramatizations of bizarre and aberrant events taken from police blotters and published in a few sentences in the daily paper, such as *Mademoiselle Fifi*. In both cases, Méténier seemed torn between wanting to shock his audiences, with or without spurts of stage blood, and proselytizing about the savage nobility of his *apaches*.

Essentially, for Méténier and his colleagues, the Theatre of the Grand Guignol, like the Théâtre Libre, was a literary and social venture. As a product of the Parisian avant-garde, it had to be ever changing and evolving. Méténier felt that he could not sustain the novelty. And, in 1898, after four seasons, he sold his interest to Max Maurey, long considered the "true" father of Grand Guignol. After 1898, Méténier disappeared into history.

Max Maurey

Max Maurey was a mystery. Not a man of the theatre, at least not known to the Montmartre crowd, Maurey was determined to make the Grand Guignol a financial success. He had little desire to attempt theatrical experimentation for its own sake; that was stuff for poets and painters. Maurey sought sure-fire formulas of terror and fear. And if Méténier focused on extreme naturalistic "slice of life" sketches, Maurey's interest pointed toward

Max Maurey

*"Horror was to be immediate and
physically shocking, even sickening."*

something different: what one critic referred to as the "slice of death" drama. Maurey's Grand Guignol was to be "pure theatre." That is, a place where every social taboo of good taste was cracked and shattered. This formula would attract the French public that slaked its blood lust and fascination with the morbid by devouring pulp novels and unlikely tabloid exposés. This clientele, in other times, flocked to country freak shows and wax museums that featured chambers of horror and sensational crime. Now, watching live realistic and gory enactments of mutilation, rape, torture, and murder, each spectator could play out his fantasies of victimization and retribution. Audiences at Maurey's Grand Guignol could truly be purged of pity and fear.

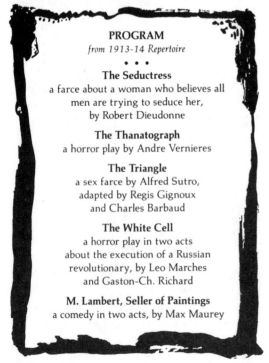

PROGRAM
from 1913-14 Repertoire
• • •
The Seductress
a farce about a woman who believes all
men are trying to seduce her,
by Robert Dieudonne

The Thanatograph
a horror play by Andre Vernieres

The Triangle
a sex farce by Alfred Sutro,
adapted by Regis Gignoux
and Charles Barbaud

The White Cell
a horror play in two acts
about the execution of a Russian
revolutionary, by Leo Marches
and Gaston-Ch. Richard

M. Lambert, Seller of Paintings
a comedy in two acts, by Max Maurey

Maurey did not abandon all of Méténier's techniques and dramatic methods. The "hot and cold shower" format (now called "laughter and tears"), if anything, became more standardized. Longer, more fully developed comedies and horror plays alternated in constant tandem. Generally, two light comedies (or farces) and two horror plays filled out an evening. The socially ironic bite of Méténier's *rosse* plays were now much more likely to be found in the comedies than in the thrillers. Horror was to be immediate and physically shocking, even sickening, usually coming in the last minutes of a horror sketch. Suspense—in the guise of psychology—replaced social and cultural sophistication.

Renowned for his perfectionism, Maurey had a habit of extensively rewriting scripts and toying constantly with the stage effects. Seated in the house with the trademark cigarette in his mouth, Maurey obsessively made each actor work and rework scenes, frequently giving them exact line-readings. The fourteen permanent performers often maintained that they, under Maurey's direction, not the audience, suffered the most at the Grand Guignol. Séverin Mars, a leading performer and popular mime, became so frustrated with Maurey's drills that he almost threw the director's table at Maurey. Another time when Maurey shouted to the pianist that he was sick of his pedestrian playing, the pianist retorted, "I'm sick of your play." The rehearsal atmosphere of barely restrained hostility and frustration probably improved the evenings' work. And in exactitude and precision, Maurey was often favorably compared to Antoine.

Maurey also had a special gift for public

AU GRAND GUIGNOL

French caricature from Rire *showing that Grand Guignol spectators
must be medically examined before entering the theatre.*

relations. One of the most famous incidents in the Grand Guignol history is recounted in a cartoon from a 1904 issue of the *Journal*. Attempting to revive his wife, who has just fainted from the shock of a Grand Guignol production, a black-frocked customer shouts for a doctor. In the theatre's foyer, Maurey replies that unfortunately the doctor too has collapsed. Although most readers passed the story off as the ultimate Grand Guignol joke, many "Guignolers" assert that an event like it actually happened at the turn of the century. Another cartoon from the same period shows an old doctor, under orders from the Police Commissioner, checking the hearts of potential Grand Guignol customers before they were allowed to enter the "House of Horror."

André de Lorde

"If anyone was responsible for the Grand Guignol's international success, it was André de Lorde, the 'Prince of Terror'."

André de Lorde

If anyone was responsible for the Grand Guignol's ascension from a local Parisian sensation to international success, it was the playwright and essayist André de Lorde, known in his lifetime as "the Prince of Terror." The son of a physician, from early age, de Lorde developed a fascination for all things frightening and morbid. Outside his father's office, the young de Lorde would listen to the sobs and screams of the patients, imagining in detail the horrifying torments they suffered. Once to rid his son of his dread and preoccupation with death, the elderly Dr. de Lorde took André to the apartment of a recently deceased man where, as a doctor, he was required to verify his departure. The young de Lorde waited outside the bedroom, watching the women in mourning passing in and out of the room, as they placed funeral candles by the side of the dead man's body. The future master of horror knew that what he envisioned in his mind's eye was even more terrifying than the sight of an actual corpse. The young de Lorde chose to remain outside. On another occasion, de Lorde's father forced the boy to keep vigil over his dead grand-mother's body on the evening before the burial. The doctor wished to convince his son, once and for all, not to be afraid of death or pain. But just the opposite happened. De Lorde became obsessed with death—especially of the horrific and painful variety. All his life, de Lorde was haunted by it.

According to his therapist and dramatic collaborator, Dr. Alfred Binet, the director of the Psychological-Physiological Laboratory of the Sorbonne, de Lorde was a poor patient, always rushing off with new plans for a play, instead of dealing with his own dark and complicated psyche. Binet often compared de Lorde to his idol, Edgar Allan Poe (always referred to by the French as Edgar Poe). Both suffered from depression and were unusually sensitive to their adolescent fears and emotions. Like many poets and writers, de Lorde possessed "the soul of a child," but in de Lorde's case, the child remained traumatized by dread.

Between 1901 and 1926, de Lorde wrote over one hundred plays of fear and horror, often in collaboration with doctors and novelists. Besides the Grand Guignol, de Lorde's plays were mounted at the Theatre

*"De Lorde wanted to write a play
so terrifying and unbearable, the entire
audience would flee from the theatre"*

Antoine (which continued in the naturalist tradition of the Théâtre Libre), the Odeon, the Théâtre Sarah Bernhardt, the Gymnase, the Vaudeville, and the Ambigu. Trained as a lawyer, de Lorde worked as a secretary to the Minister of Finance and later received an appointment as a chief librarian at the Bibliothèque de l'Arsenal. More than any previous writer for the Grand Guignol, de Lorde was a literary man, giving interviews to newspapers and magazines, publishing volumes of his horror plays, even writing manifestoes and explanations of his work.

In one preface to a collection of plays, de Lorde stated that men who flee fear through the day, flock to it after sundown at the Grand Guignol. The horror play was an essential feature of modern life as the gladiator contests, *autos-da-fè*, and guillotine beheadings had been in other times. And identifying with his American predecessor,

de Lorde wanted to create one of Poe's dreams: to write a play so terrifying and unbearable that several minutes after the curtain rises, the entire audience would flee from the theatre en masse.

An avid reader and student of all the newest trends in psychology and criminal behavior, de Lorde was the first dramatist to set plays in operating rooms and insane asylums. As a playwright, he mastered the two principles vital to affective terror: creating plots where the suspense continues to grow until the gruesome finale unfolds; and, the very opposite trick, preparing the audience for an inevitable conclusion they have already guessed. Either way, the audience's anticipation of horror was the key—otherwise the terrifying and sickening conclusions would merely draw simple surprise or even laughter.

The collaboration of Maurey and de Lorde turned the Grand Guignol into an elite social entertainment despite the bloody climaxes and horrific violence. Just as Méténier had used the Grand Guignol to perfect his own brand of sordid "slice of life" sketches to educate Parisian audiences how the underclass lived and thought, de Lorde had invented a new dramatic genre devoted to "slices of death." It spoke to mankind's universal dread. And society women, in particular, were drawn to it. The presence of attending doctors at the theatre was no longer a publicity stunt. Spectators fainted on the average of two per night. Interestingly, it was mainly male playgoers who swooned, probably because, unlike their female escorts, the men failed to cover their eyes during the horrifying moments.

Even the bloodless, *rosse*-type plays produced shocks in the audience. The famous

*"Spectators fainted on the average
of two per night."*

British travel critic, F. Berkeley Smith reported on one such reaction in the winter of 1902. After a Grand Guignol performance of the relatively mild *An Affair of Morals*, the spectators, having already laughed heartily at the previous play, a sex farce, became rigid when two prostitute characters marched the dead judge's body out of a restaurant singing the "Fireman's Anthem."

As the curtain fell, the audience seemed in a stupor. A woman beside me sat staring at the floor, crying. Men coughed and remained silent. Not until the pianist in the foyer struck up a lively polka did they leave their seats for a little cognac and a breath of air.   —How Paris Amuses Itself
                            (NY and London, 1903)

Under Maurey's direction and continual publicity, the Grand Guignol was newly recognized as a unique French entertainment. Parisian guidebooks in every language recommended it. After the Eiffel Tower— but equally with the *maisons de tolerance* (the legalized brothels), Maxim's, and the Louvre—the Theatre of the Grand Guignol had become the best known tourist attraction in Paris by 1910.

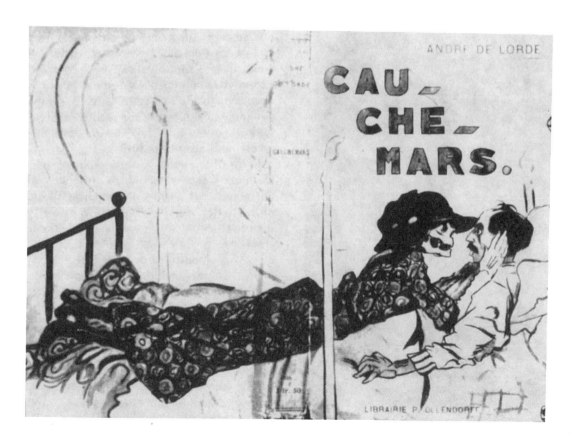

*"At the very height of the scenic action
and the character's emotional displays,
hidden trick properties had
to be executed perfectly."*

Camille Choisy

In 1915 Maurey retired. Camille Choisy, a small well-groomed man with extravagant taste—he wore a ring on each finger—took over in a partnership with the Rumanian-born, Charles Zibell. Choisy, a true *homme du théâtre*, was himself a character actor in second-rate theatres and a sympathetic personality. In writing about the new regime, however, Antoine, now an important arbiter of theatrical taste, felt that the Grand Guignol had used up its novelty. The

Camille Choisy

First World War, then settling into the unheroic posture of trench warfare, had introduced a new realism and horror in life. But, for Choisy, the technology of death helped enlarge his hideous vocabulary of torture and death: poison gas, explosive devices, electrical cables, surgical instruments and drills replaced the old pistol, dagger, and primitive sword.

Actually, the Grand Guignol reached its artistic apogee after the First World War. Its familiar array of acting techniques that once showed off a heightened realism—within gruesome circumstances—now transformed itself into a particular and discernible style of performance. Instead of the single-minded, Antoine-like naturalism in the creation of character and action, a more colorful and complicated behavior was expected from the players under Choisy. According to a 1923 press release, the Grand Guignol actors present "the realities of life—with its ardours, its violences, its enchantments, and also its beauties."

More than ever, Grand Guignol performers were expected to inhabit real characters with a full range of powerful and animalistic impulses—as they secretly manipulated the catches on fleshy prosthetic creations, intricate spring contraptions, and a host of blood-filled devices. Naturally, it was at the very height of the scenic action and the characters' emotional displays that the hidden trick properties had to be executed perfectly. When a beaker of fuming vitriol was unexpectedly thrown into the face of a character by his lover, a look of horror had to register on the actor's face at the same moment his skin transmogrified into a smoking, bubbling, and cracked mass of ooze. The smallest manual

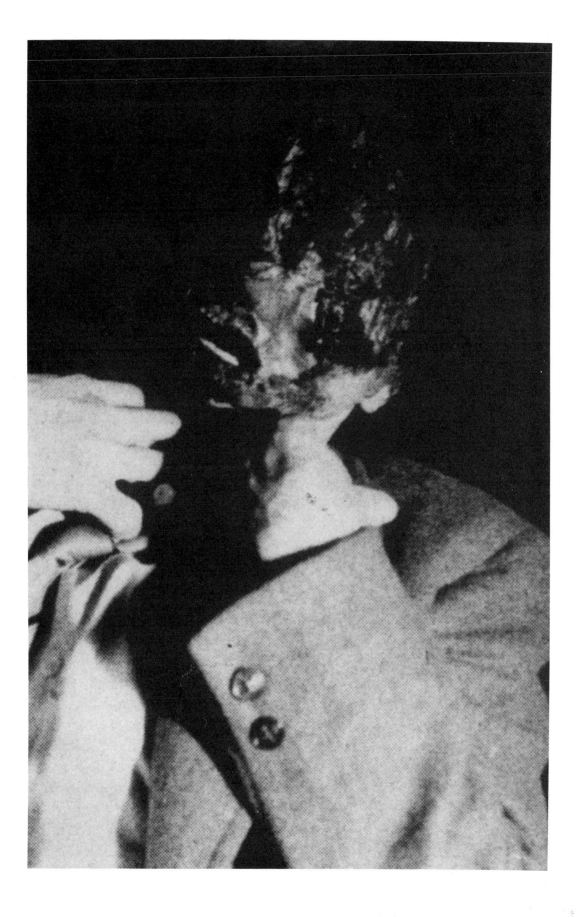

*"Maxa cried 'Help!' 983 times,
'Murderer!' 1,263 times, and
'Rape!' 1,804 and one-half times."*

Maxa

slip or false note in the acting could thoroughly ruin a twenty-minute scenario. Each Grand Guignol actor had to possess a double skill in stage concentration and sleight-of-hand trickery. And the French audiences of the teens and twenties became excited since they had a new yardstick by which to judge Choisy's productions.

The most celebrated performer during the Grand Guignol's heyday was Maxa, known in the newspapers as "the High Priestess of the Temple of Horror." A glamorous actress with an instinctive understanding of the macabre, Maxa was said to have played all of her roles as if she "were carrying a torch." During her relatively brief career, she was murdered more than 10,000 times and in some 60 ways. A few examples: devoured by a ravenous puma, cut into 93 pieces and glued back together, smashed by

a roller-compressor, burnt alive, cut open by a traveling salesman who wanted her intestines; she was also raped over 3,000 times under a dozen circumstances. Camillo Antona-Traversi, Choisy's secretary and an early historian of the Grand Guignol, calculated that on the stage, Maxa cried "Help!" 983 times, "Murderer!" 1,263 times, and "Rape!" 1,804 and 1/2 times. In her memoirs, Maxa wrote about the value of timing; a line or gesture said too fast, or slow, could easily ruin the tension built up over ten or fifteen minutes and destroy the evening.

Choisy encouraged the work of new playwrights by not rewriting each and every scene—at least not until after opening night. Maurey rarely extended that courtesy to dramatists and often had problems retaining their services after one or two experiences with his style of Grand Guignol. Yet even with the difficulties they created for their playwrights and adapters, both directors ultimately preserved and encouraged the writing of one-act plays, an art that quickly faded after Symbolism's collapse before World War One. Choisy also intensified the Grand Guignol atmosphere by going to extra lengths for verisimilitude in set design. The scenic environments for Choisy's productions often consisted of modern ships, blimps, submarines, railroad cars, factories, and mines. Consequently, the naturalistic settings grew considerably in fantastic and expensive detail.

Of course, the public's actual reaction to the Grand Guignol shockers ran the gamut from outright revulsion to ironic detachment and playful amusement. For premieres, audiences often attended in evening dresses and tuxedos, bringing their own champagne

*"Resident millionaires and royalty from
every continent attended regularly."*

and glasses. Resident millionaires from every continent, and royalty and their families came regularly. Among the best-known "Guignolers" in the Choisy-era were the King of Greece, Princess Wilhemina of Holland, the Sultan of Morocco's sons and daughters, and the wife of the deposed King Alfonso XIII, who invariably arrived on All Saint's Eve. When King Carol of Rumania was forced into exile with his red-haired mistress, Magda Lupesco, they publicly appeared at the Grand Guignol in Paris. And, after the tables turned in Rumanian politics, the King's pretender Prince Nichols fled to France and, like his father, was taken in by the murderous antics of the Grand Guignol. Still lesser types made up the bulk of the audiences. One such devoted patron was the Vietnamese political refugee, Ho Chi Minh, then a noodle and pastry cook at a Chinese restaurant.

The involvement of some playgoers was so strong that they sometimes shouted, "Assassin!" at the various "villains," just as their forbears did in the 1830s Boulevard du Crime melodramas. "Guignolers" liked to repeat the number of times that the house physician was called to treat temporarily sickened spectators. At one performance, six people passed out when an actress, whose eyeball was just gouged out, re-entered the stage, revealing a gooey, blood-encrusted hole in her skull. Backstage, the actors themselves calculated their success accord-

"Jouvin's plays mixed psychological and sexual menace within the traditional crime and laboratory formats."

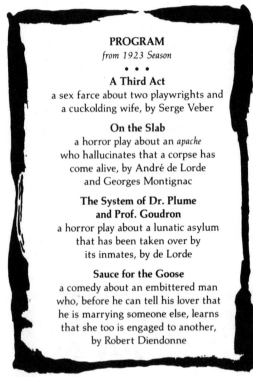

PROGRAM

from 1923 Season

• • •

A Third Act

a sex farce about two playwrights and
a cuckolding wife, by Serge Veber

On the Slab

a horror play about an *apache*
who hallucinates that a corpse has
come alive, by André de Lorde
and Georges Montignac

**The System of Dr. Plume
and Prof. Goudron**

a horror play about a lunatic asylum
that has been taken over by
its inmates, by de Lorde

Sauce for the Goose

a comedy about an embittered man
who, before he can tell his lover that
he is marrying someone else, learns
that she too is engaged to another,
by Robert Diendonne

ing to the evening's faintings. During one de Lorde horror play that ended with a realistic blood transfusion, a record was set: fifteen playgoers had lost consciousness. Between sketches, the cobble-stoned alley outside the theatre was frequented by hyperventilating couples and vomiting individuals.

Jack Jouvin

Charles Zibell, having lost most of his fortune during the war and in the inflation that followed, sold his share of the Grand Guignol to the playwright, director, and producer Jack Jouvin in 1926. Jouvin's uneasy collaboration with Choisy only lasted three years. Choisy departed in 1928 and, within a year, opened the rival *Théâtre du*

Rire et de L'Epouvante ("Theatre of Laughter and Fright") at the Varietés Theatre under the direction of Jacques Albert.

Maxa, too, fired by Jouvin (supposedly because of her personal success in drawing an independent following of "Guignolers"), started her own terror-and-comedy type playhouse in the Montmartre, "The Theatre of Vice and Virtue." Yet, despite a superior repertoire and style of acting, neither Choisy or Maxa's theatres lasted more than a few seasons. The copyrighted name of "Grand Guignol" proved to be an attraction of its own.

In 1930, Jouvin announced a new Grand Guignol repertoire. He played down the de Lorde tradition of physical violence and flesh-searing torture, retaining only three of the Prince's masterpieces altogether. Jouvin's modern horror plays mixed psychological and sexual menace within the traditional crime and laboratory formats. Mental cruelty, homosexuality, hysteria, unexpected betrayal, and suspense fueled the plots. Most of the silly sex farces were eliminated. Even the "hot shower" comedies became less bawdy and physical. Jouvin created unifying themes for the programs, such as staging an evening of comedies and horror plays all authored by the same writer. Under the pseudonyms of Edmond Gilbert and S. Ramel, Jouvin wrote many of these dramas himself. It was all to no avail.

In the early and middle thirties, the Grand Guignol lost its novelty and appeal—except to American tourists and French university students out for a hoot. The theatre's balcony proved to be an ideal and daring place to engage in necking sessions and more pronounced sex play. In addition, Hollywood sound films, like *Dracula* and *Frankenstein*,

"In the early and middle thirties, the Grand Guignol lost its novelty and appeal."

Theatre of Laughter and Fright
PROGRAM
Premiere, February 8th, 1929
• • •
One Night of Edgar Poe
a horror play, by André de Lorde

Harmony
a comedy in three scenes,
by Henri Duvernois

Destination Unknown
a horror play in two acts and four
scenes, by Bernard Zimmer

The Moroccan Breakfast
a comedy, by Jules Romains

PROGRAM
from the 1932 Season
• • •
The Need for Youthfulness
a comedy, by Edmond Gilbert
(Jack Jouvin)

Zanzibar
a horror play, by J. de Heeckeren

Sexuality
a horror play in three scenes,
by S. Ramel (J. Jouvin)

Neither Dandia Nor Boubouroche
a comedy, by E. Gilbert
(J. Jouvin)

borrowing the very techniques of terror and laughter from the Grand Guignol, became fierce competition. Only the ubiquitous glistening-red stage blood that still splattered and flowed in pailfuls caught the spectators' attention differently.

Eva Berkson

In 1937, the dynamic British-born actress Eva Berkson bought out Jouvin and invigorated the old vehicle. Even Maxa returned briefly to once again be stabbed, burnt, scalded, shot, and torn to bits. During an episode of prolonged screaming, however, Maxa seemed to have permanently damaged her vocal cords; her audio range was forever reduced to normal speaking level. Intermixing some of the oldest farces with up-to-date horror plays, Berkson seemed to have found the perfect formula. She even mounted a horror play in 1939 that dealt with Nazi atrocities in Poland. The Grand Guignol flourished until the German invasion in 1940. With other British nationals, Berkson fled to England and waited out the war there, joining a women's auxiliary to the R.A.F.

During the Nazi occupation of Paris, the Grand Guignol found a familiar spectator, the non-French-speaking spectator. Most of the repertoire reverted to Choisy's old bills and the theatre became very popular with the enemy troops. Hermann Goering in particular enjoyed the productions; but, for the Gestapo and the SS elite, the Grand Guignol—with its gratuitous violence and lewd pornographic interludes—was a penultimate example of *Entartete Kunst* ("Degenerate Art"). Nazi censors vainly attempted to ban the popular French decadent entertainment. Only when German victory was assured,

*"Documentary footage of Nazi death camps
shown in neighborhood movie houses
became impossible competition."*

it was declared, could the Grand Guignol be liquidated and excised from the culture of New Europe.

One year after the Allied liberation of Paris in 1944, Berkson returned with her husband, Alexander Dundas, to piece together her beloved Grand Guignol. Initially, among the newly patriotic French theatre-goers, there was some resentment against the Theatre of Horror and Terror, although these ill-feelings paled when compared with their real hatred toward the "legitimate" theatres, revue-houses, and cabarets that regularly entertained Nazi troops. Choisy, who kept the Grand Guignol running profitably during the Nazi occupation, fortunately died before the Committee of Liberation got around to trying him for wartime collaboration.

As a returning Englishwoman and a wife of an R.A.F. pilot, Berkson did not need to exonerate her wartime activities. Besides, the current occupiers of Europe, the Americans, took to the Grand Guignol themselves. When General George Patton, on leave from his German headquarters, visited it one evening, a French newspaper headlined "'Old Blood and Guts' at the Grand Guignol." The next day, excited audiences queued up for tickets, thinking that a new play had just opened.

The postwar years were difficult for Berkson. The Second World War, unlike the First, left the Grand Guignol's potential viewers hungry for hideous events—but real ones, not those imagined by Montmartre playwrights. Hundreds of sensational books and magazines describing the Nazi tortures and massacres were pinned up on the posts of the book kiosks along the Seine. Documentary footage of the Nazi death camps

and medical experiments on humans that was shown in neighborhood movie houses became impossible competition. Audiences guffawed or laughed at de Lorde's pseudo-atrocities at the Grand Guignol. In 1947, Berkson confessed, "I've come to the conclusion that the only way to frighten a French audience since the war is to cut up a woman on stage—a live woman, of course—and throw them the pieces!" She tried several new formulas, including full-length dramatizations of foreign novels. These, although superb and terrifyingly produced, only worked for a time. The ageless, former actress retired in 1951.

Eva Berkson

"By 1959, a camp quality had overtaken the Grand Guignol performances."

The Last Years of the Grand Guignol

Between 1951 and 1954, Charles Nonon, company manager, took over temporarily under the ownership of Max Maurey's sons, Denis and Michel. Nonon also attempted various formulas, now including full-length satires and even music revues. Again, the performances were good, but the Grand Guignol began to lose its special identity.

From 1954 to 1958, the crime writer and feminist journalist, Raymonde Machard took over and improved the reputation of the Grand Guignol dramatically. For one, she used better and younger writers. Yet, the acting finally suffered, becoming sloppy and occasionally dangerous. One actress almost hanged herself in a leather contraption; another was badly burnt during an incineration scene. Still one more had a nervous breakdown on stage.

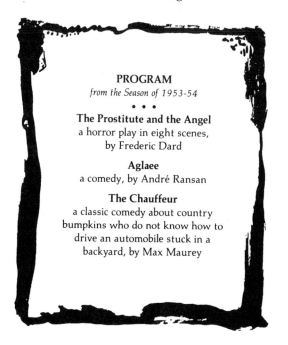

PROGRAM
from the Season of 1953-54
• • •
The Prostitute and the Angel
a horror play in eight scenes,
by Frederic Dard

Aglaee
a comedy, by André Ransan

The Chauffeur
a classic comedy about country
bumpkins who do not know how to
drive an automobile stuck in a
backyard, by Max Maurey

Some critics believed that this had to do with a "New Realism" in the acting, but a few of the events were pure hocus-pocus: like the publicity stunt where a Grand Guignol actress, playing a character who was kidnapped in *No Orchids for Miss Blandish*, disappeared herself and was declared held for ransom before opening night. Yet a number of the Grand Guignol's "problems" in the fifties could not be faked. The playwright of *The Machine to Kill Life* actually did die on opening night. And the technical adviser for a 1956 play about a Le Mans race car wreck, *The Death of Ralenti*, was one of 71 who died that year in a Le Mans disaster.

By 1959, when Fred Pasquale replaced Machard, a camp quality had overtaken the Grand Guignol performances. The audiences consisted of 50% tourists and many of the French fans were cheering on the stage madmen. In 1961, Nonon once again assumed the directorship. Despite horrific effects—like the tips of a woman's nipples being snipped off with a hedge shears followed by a gouging of her eyes (they were scooped out with a soup spoon and jack-knife)—the Grand Guignol itself was dying. Nonon lamented that "We could never equal Buchenwald. Before the war, everyone felt that what was happening on stage was impossible. Now we know that these things, and worse, are possible in reality."

In November 1962, the Theatre of the Grand Guignol closed its doors. The naughty joke, which once attracted the attentions of Paris' elite, now had gone stale and soft. It also became financially hopeless. Small-scale pornographic versions of the Grand Guignol in other theatres and nightclubs had already captured the bulk of

German and British tourists wandering through Pigalle. The playhouse on Rue Chapel temporarily reopened as Theatre 347, featuring a repertoire of science fantasy plays. But, in March 1963, with much fanfare, the building that housed the Grand Guignol was totally destroyed—comically, somewhat in the manner that a harmless but aging vampire is dispatched in bad films. A squad of bereted laborers, hoisting picks and shovels, grinned, then struck with their primitive implements at the weak and ancient facade. Second-string journalists and newsreel cameramen, ironically about to be forcibly retired themselves, captured the final *coup de grâce*. The Grand Guignol as a French institution died in 1963, but, only, as the "Guignolers" then claimed, to be replaced by something else. Interestingly, Nonon and several of the Grand Guignol performers went into the restaurant trade.

PROGRAM
from an Evening of the 1962 Season
• • •
Parody of Death
a horror play in two acts,
from Peter Randa's novel,
adapted by Maurice Renay

Eyes Without a Face
a horror play in two acts,
from Jean Redon's novel,
adapted by Renay

Two Women in Power
a comedy in two acts, by J. Marevu

THE INFLUENCE OF
THE GRAND GUIGNOL

HE GRAND GUIGNOL HAS LONG BEEN considered a unique French entertainment. Although it attracted a large international audience to its Montmartre lair and appeared prominently in foreign-language guidebooks of the City of Light between 1905 and 1940, the Theatre of the Grand Guignol itself was a poor export. Under Maurey's direction, the Parisian performers played successfully across France in summer months but in the spring of 1908, their first tour to London ended in a financial disaster. The political rivalry between the two leading colonial powers was at its height, and British critics savaged the Gaullic shockers as "mild amusement." A similar fate befell the tour in Berlin and Rome.

In the early twenties, Choisy's troupe traveled to Rio de Janeiro, Montreal, and New York. These ventures too often ended with short seasons and poor notices. Foreign play reviewers, who seemed to like neither the terror dramas nor the sex farces, had a greater sway and affect on the tastes of the local audiences than their equally critical Parisian counterparts.

Theatre

Only in French-speaking Montreal did Choisy find sold-out houses and an enthusiastic following. The theatre critic of the *Montreal Herald* (October 9th, 1923) summed up the fervent reception of his fellow Quebequoise:

> *The work of the Grand Guignol is like nothing else in the world of theatre. It is devoted to the visualization of a pitiless analysis and dissection of the elemental human emotions, but it mainly concerns itself with the psychology of fear, terror, horror, and the reaction of the human conscience and the human need to influence both real and imaginary, working in and through certain suggestive atmospheric environments and upon the retina of imagination. It absorbs the attention of the beholder utterly.*

Just one week later at New York's Frolic Theatre, a diminutive playhouse over the New Amsterdam Theatre, the same French-speaking troupe and its repertoire were met with a different reaction. Critics of all the major newspapers found problems with the Grand Guignol's acting, *mise en scène*, and writing. The Selwyns, who produced the ten-

THE SELWYNS PRESENT
THE GRAND GUIGNOL PLAYERS
TO AMERICA
PREMIÈRE PERFORMANCE
MONDAY EVENING, OCT. 15TH 1923
AT THE FROLIC THEATRE
IN NEW YORK CITY

*"The Grand Guignol experience seemed to
be limited to the physical confines of the
French-speaking world."*

week season in Manhattan, may have over-
sold the theatrical novelty, calling it an "even
greater event than the coming of the
Moscow Art Theatre," which played to
frenzied American spectators the previous
year. Typically, *The New York Tribune* (October
16, 1923) characterized the evening as
"respectable, and not particularly flesh-
creeping."

For a week's program, Alla Nazimova, the
Stanislavsky-trained Hollywood starlet,
joined the Grand Guignol. Having been
banned from the Keith Vaudeville Circuit
in a contract dispute over her suggestive
sketch, *The Unknown*, the Russian femme
fatale's notoriety should have brought in
crowds of curiosity seekers and fans but,
largely because of critical pressures, did not.
The Selwyns' grandiose project closed
somewhat ignominiously after five difficult
weeks. The Grand Guignol experience,
despite the multi-lingual and cosmopolitan
nature of its audiences in Paris, seemed to
be limited to the physical confines of the
French-speaking world.

A few Grand Guignol playwrights, like
de Lorde and Sartène, savored a growing
international popularity as their dramas
were translated (or adapted) into a dozen
European languages, as well as Japanese and
Hebrew. Most of these foreign-language
versions, however, were mounted in evenings of assorted short plays in an effort to
preserve the art of the one-act play. Rarely
were the Grand Guignol sketches successful
in and of themselves. Often the horrific
effects became muted or were edited out
completely.

In 1913 at the Princess Theatre in New
York, the celebrated American actor and
director, Holbrook Blin, introduced Grand

Guignol plays into his second season of the
Princess Players. Adapted to emphasize their
mysterious and occult features, rather than
the traditional gruesome or shock value,
even horror plays like *Hari-Kari*, *Room Number
Six*, and *The Kiss in the Dark* appeared vapid
and greatly resembled the accompanying
American mystery dramas given by the
Princess Players. Then, four years after the
Selwyn fiasco, George Renavent established
the American Grand Guignol, Inc. at the
Grove Street Theatre in Greenwich Village
in December 1927. This and other efforts,
during the next five years, at the Temple

Theatre, the Palace, and the Chanin Auditorium rarely lasted a complete season. The last venture, in the best Grand Guignol style, advertised the presence of a doctor and nurse—and mortician, if necessary—at every performance. Still, in the twenties and thirties, an avid American spectator seeking the true Grand Guignol would have to cross the Atlantic. (Other American Grand Guignol imitations surfaced briefly in Pittsburgh, New York, and Los Angeles in the post World War Two era.)

Outside of Paris, only two Grand Guignol theatres attained a noted degree of success.

Jose Levy

The first, located at Rome's Teatro Metastasio began under Alfredo Sainati's directorship as the result of the Parisian Grand Guignol tour in 1908. Although challenged by a rival group, "The Grand Guignol International" in 1910 and 1911, the original Roman Grand Guignol prospered, staging both Italian versions of the Grand Guignol classics and indigenous shockers. Among the many talented writers that Sainati managed to attract to his energetic ensemble was Luigi Chiarelli, the doyen of the Italian School of the Grotesque. Here the Italians diverged from their French colleagues with a heavy theatrical emphasis on social and metaphysical problems. Grotesque comedy blended effortlessly with grisly attacks on the social order. The Italian Grand Guignol theatre performed uninterrupted from 1923 to 1928.

In 1920, Jose Levy opened a Grand Guignol theatre at London's Little Theatre, a small playhouse tucked away from the central Strand district. Obsessed with producing a theatre of terror north of the Channel long before World War One intervened, Levy finally managed to engage the services of one of England's great acting families: the Thorndike-Cassons. Sybil Thorndike, soon to create the part of George Bernard Shaw's Saint Joan, acted with a truth of character and feeling that few British actresses had exhibited since Sarah Siddons performed Lady Macbeth in 1782.

Like Maxa, Sybil Thorndike suffered every torment and humiliation that the British Grand Guignol could invent, being crushed by a collapsible ceiling; murdered and stuffed into a trunk; blinded and strangled; terrified as her husband was

"Sybil Thorndike sought realistic images to feed her supernatural acting needs."

Sybil Thorndike

tossed to a ravenous band of wolfdogs; and encased in a block of plaster. Thorndike sought realistic images to feed her supernatural acting needs. She discovered that spiders rested their bodies and psyches while their simple musculature remained rigid. In a Georgian diary, she found a reference to a man who became helpless after falling into a wagon filled with thorns; "every nerve almost strained to a violent degree." These were her inspirations for Grand Guignol acting. Russell Thorndike, Sybil's brother, compared performing at Levy's theatre to a powerful kind of religious confession. He claimed that it even cured him of an unending and hideous stream of nightmares that plagued him for years, all of which returned unfortunately when the British Grand Guignol folded in 1923.

Both adaptations of traditional Grand Guignol classics and newly written horror plays and comedies formed the core of Levy's

"The overall mad feeling of the German Expressionist film had less to do with Expressionism from the German stage than the influence of the Grand Guignol."

Grand Guignol. As devoted as the British actors were, the public censors felt even more strongly about the theatre. While most newspaper critics praised the work of the Little Theatre, others attacked its unwholesome qualities such as setting a sketch in a lavatory. Actually, the play *G.H.Q Love*, took place in a cloak room outside the clearly-marked W.C.s for men and women. No matter. Other institutions quickly followed suit. The Society for the Prevention of Cruelty to Animals complained about the backstage torturing of wolfhounds to achieve the sound effects for *The Kill*. In fact, it was the actors' lungs that suffered since the howling yelps were produced by blowing furiously into glass pipes. Posters of the Grand Guignol were banned from London's underground trains, owing to their "immoral" nature. In the end, the success of Levy's Grand Guignol brought about its

British Grand Guignol
PROGRAM
Premiere, September 1st, 1920

• • •

How to Be Happy
a morality play, by Pierre Verber

G.H.Q. Love
a drama by Sewell Collins,
adapted from Pierre Rehm's play

The Hand of Death
a horror play, by André de Lorde
and Alfred Binet

Oh, Hell!
a "revuette", by Reginald Arkell
and Russell Thorndike

downfall. Sybil Thorndike, her husband Lewis Casson, Russell Thorndike, and several other performers, by 1923, were too well known for the arcane venture and finally were lured into more legitimate avenues of theatre.

Motion Pictures

The Grand Guignol's most significant influence on world culture can be found in the popular sub-genres of the Hollywood film. While the scary phantasmagoric style and primitive psychological thriller existed from the very beginnings of the European motion picture industry, the Grand Guignol had a major impact on their look and development by the end of World War One. De Lorde himself scripted eleven silent movies in France between 1911 and 1914, including a cinematic short of *The System of Dr. Plume and Prof. Goudron*. In fact, the hideous ironies of plot and character, unexpected brutalities, and overall mad feeling of the German Expressionist film had less to do with Expressionism from the German stage than the influence of the Grand Guignol.

Robert Oswald, the indefatigable Berlin film director, formally introduced Grand Guignol plots in his two film anthologies, *Unearthly Stories* (1919) and *Five Unearthly Stories* (1933). *The Cabinet of Dr. Caligari* (1920), the keynote German Expressionist film, actually was rejected by Expressionist writers in a series of bitter manifestoes as an alien example of Expressionist style and philosophy. Hypnotic spells; the ultimate superiority of wicked, insane authority over bourgeois power; gratuitous violence; the frailty of love were the characteristic features of the Grand Guignol, not German

Prop hands and feet filled with bulbs of stage blood, circa 1938.

istic," terms that accurately defined the real Grand Guignol. Both in the silent and sound eras, Todd Browning created the films that borrowed most heavily from the Theatre of the Grand Guignol. Especially in *The Unholy Three* (1925), *The Unknown* (1928), *Freaks* (1932), and *The Devil Doll* (1936), Browning established a particular, unhealthy atmosphere that closely resembled pure grand-guignolesque. Lon Chaney, John Barrymore, Bela Lugosi, Peter Lorre, Boris Karloff, and Charles Laughton all personified the acting styles that Choisy and his troupe perfected in the twenties. Finally, in 1935, Karl Freund, the celebrated ex-patriot German cameraman, as a kind of recognition, directed a Peter Lorre vehicle, *Mad Love*, that utilized a Grand Guignol setting for his remake of "The Hands of Orlac" story.

After *Mad Love*, however, the Grand Guignol as a cultural icon disappeared from Hollywood. And with it went all its stepchildren. By the end of the thirties, vampires, zombie-masters, lunatics, werewolves, insane scientists and their vengeful creations became the subjects of silly parodies and low-grade shockers. Sadistic Gestapo officers and puffy-faced Southern sheriffs now satisfied Hollywood's thirst for perverse and monstrous archetypes. Curiously, American radio picked up the dramatic outcasts. By 1939, the Grand Guignol and its plots showed up repeatedly on Arch Obler's phenomenally successful horror series *Lights Out!* as well as in its many broadcast imitations like *The Haunting Hour*, *The Weird Dr. Strange*, *The Creaking Door*, and *Inner Sanctum* (which mixed low-comedy and terror like the original Grand Guignol).

Occasional anthology films, emphasizing horror and occult, appeared in Great Britain

Expressionism. Only the frame of a dreamer's nightmare over the core of the *Caligari* plot, tacked on late in the production, along with the decor and acting style exhibited theatrical Expressionism's attributes.

In Hollywood, the "old dark house" mysteries of the silent era, like Paul Leni's *The Cat and Canary* (1927) and horror spectacles like *Phantom of the Opera* (1925), owed much more to the Grand Guignol than Expressionism. In 1928, Robert Florey directed the first acknowledged Hollywood-Grand Guignol film, *The Film Coffin*, which was criticized as "queer" and "impression-

*"American directors in the
mid-70's developed their own
Grand-Guignol-like sub-genre."*

and France in the immediate postwar years but not until the technicolor and three-dimensional splash of Vincent Price and Christopher Lee monster movies in the fifties and early sixties did the horrific find its way back into the commercial cinema. Unhealthy black comedies that revealed the gothic undertrappings of contemporary life, like Alfred Hitchcock's *Psycho* (1960) and Richard Aldridge's *What Ever Happened to Baby Jane?* (1962) surfaced in the same period and led Hollywood back into the filmic grand-guignolesque. The height (or low point) of the kids-slashed-by-an-insane-avenger format was reached in the mid-seventies when young independent American directors developed their own Grand Guignol-like sub-genre. (Herschell Gordon Lewis originated the sickening "we can see your organs" film with the 1963 *Blood Feast*.) In France, the Grand Guignol settings appeared in two major films, *The Seduction of a Vampire* (1967) and *Grand Guignol* (1986). More than anything else, the later movie attempted to find an accomodation of psychological terror from the traditional *film noir* genre with an historical appreciation of the Grand Guignol's waning days.

Herschell Gordon Lewis' *Blood Feast*

STAGE TRICKS OF THE GRAND GUIGNOL

NTIL 1939, MOST OF THE SCENIC techniques, including the bloody stage tricks, of the Grand Guignol were a tightly guarded secret. A number of them were even patented. The secrecy probably had more to do with concealing their simplicity of design than a desire to prevent other theatres from using them. The Grand Guignol audiences wanted to believe in the reality of the gory stage actions, and, therefore, by their shocked reactions unconsciously assisted in the life-like presentations of grisly murders, torture, corporal mutilation, and bleeding wounds.

Following Antoine's naturalistic formula for exact, realistic detail, many of the Grand Guignol's frightening techniques were little more than well crafted stage trickery. The manager of the Grand Guignol, Paul Ratineau, known as the "Third Bandit of Horror" (after de Lorde and Choisy), invented ingenious devices to create the sound of a harsh rain storm or a creaking door. He discovered the further away the sound source was from the audience, the more effective (or chilling) it was. Choisy spent whole days just orchestrating the sound design and lighting effects of a production. At the Grand Guignol, scenic atmosphere was as important as the acting and plot in an evening. From the time the curtain arose, a special sensation of strangeness and mystery had to envelope the audience. In part, this was caused by a shadowing effect in the overhead lights and an imperceptible, hazy illumination of red and green colors in the corners of the proscenium. According to Maxa, the partially darkened stage decor produced an unconscious shock in the spectator: something was about to happen, something hidden was about to appear from the shadows.

The Grand Guignol adhered to Dracula's biblical dictum: "Blood is the life!" Their single most celebrated secret involved patented blood recipes. Although varieties of stage blood have existed at least since the time of the classical Roman theatre, the Grand Guignol made something of a fetish of them. A dark, sticky stage blood signified old wounds; a lighter, dripping fluid showed new ones. The standard formula consisted mostly of a heated mixture of carmine and glycerin. Combined daily in a cauldron, the crimson liquid flowed like blood but also coagulated after a few minutes to form scabs. In quiet moments,

"Daggers with retractable blades spurted blood when the blood-filled handles were squeezed."

spectators could sometimes hear the property woman whisper backstage, "Edmond, hurry! Warm up the blood." But because of the extensive cleaning bills in later years, even the use of the famous blood compounds followed a rule-of-thumb direction: Large body wounds were limited to women (smaller costumes to clean) and head wounds for men (less hair to clean).

The most famous tricks of the Grand Guignol involved the realistic execution of violent actions and instantaneous sleight of hand transformation. Daggers with retractable blades spurted blood when the blood-filled handles were squeezed. Dying victims could reveal throat and facial wounds by tracing their blood-soaked fingers over the imagined area. Sword or knife wielding murderers could seemingly penetrate their victims' limbs by using a stage weapon with an empty curved clasp between the handle and blade. Out of nowhere, lunatics could suddenly foam at the mouth simply by chewing on a hidden bit of soap. Mirrors, facial masks, concealed rubber pieces for wounds and burns, fake heads and limbs, all the paraphernalia of magicians, when expertly used—during moments of darkness or out of the spectators' view—created an atmosphere of sickening and eerie realism. Nonon frequently purchased different animal eyeballs from taxidermists—not only for visual realism, when characters eye's were gouged out, but for the organs' ability to bounce when they hit the stage floor.

Staging for the "Ribbon of Flesh" Torture
from The Garden of Torture *by* Pierre Chaine *(1922)*

Before Ti-Bah's second entrance, prepare the following back stage: On Ti-Bah's back, at the level of her shoulder blades, affix a thin strip of adhesive plaster colored red on the bottom and flesh-color on top.

When Han says: "I said it," Li-Chang grabs Ti-Bah, forces her to her knees and, facing the audience, tears off her shirt.

As soon as Han gives the knife to Ti-Mao, Li-Chang, with one knee to the ground next to Ti-Bah, holds her wrists with one hand and with the other grabs her by the hair and pulls her head down.

Ti-Mao uses this moment to simulate making two slits in her back. In reality, he bloodies her back with fake blood contained in a small tube or vial, which he then hides.

As soon as Ti-Mao has finished this preparation, Li-Chang pushes down on the back of Ti-Bah's neck, forcing her forehead to the ground, thereby exposing her back to the audience.

At the same time, Ti-Mao seizes the top end of the plaster and tears it very slowly down her back so that everyone has time to see the bloody scrap peel off of Ti-Bah's shoulders.

CONCLUSION

QUESTION ALWAYS ARISES WITH the Grand Guignol: Why study it? Other than treating it as some gross-out joke of theatre history. Although the Grand Guignol seemed to have greatly influenced other theatres and genres, what could make it a worthwhile theatre of its own? The answer is one that becomes more and more important in contemporary and popular art: Censorship and gratuitous violence and sex in art.

In the United States, millions of otherwise liberal, "right-thinking," adults oppose government censorship in the arts, especially motion pictures, unless gratuitous violence is involved. On that issue, they frequently take an inflexible stand: violence on stage or screen can lead children or others into anti-social, physical activity. Gestapo agents in Paris believed much the same thing. During the heyday of the Grand Guignol, in the 1920s and 1930s, there was probably less violent crime on the street or by the state in Paris than in any major European capital. The reverse situation was true in Nazi Germany, where theatre and film censorship achieved its glory. Does that imply then that the Grand Guignol relieved its Parisian public of violent impulses, that it "purged" them of fear and pity? Probably not. Only that the relationship between violence in art and its affects on human behavior is rooted firmly in individual cultures. The connections between what people see and what they do is not clearly manifested, except to compulsive censors of art. Each particular culture informs its children differently. Sometimes, barbaric stage activity only produces health-giving chills and laughter. Such was the case of the Grand Guignol.

Selected Bibliography

"Le bazar de la terror," *Voilà* (Paris), October 20th, 1939.

Camillo Antona-Traversi, *L'Histoire du Grand Guignol* (Paris, 1933).

Comoedia Illustré (Paris): July 1913; January 1914; September 1920; July 1922; May 1st, 1924; and 15 June 1924.

Frantisek Deak, "The Grand Guignol," *The Drama Review* (NY), March 1974.

Daniel Gerould, "Oscar Méténier and *Comedie Rosse*," *The Drama Review* (NY), Spring 1984.

Grand Guignol Annual Review (London, 1921).

"Grand Guignol" Files of the Bibliothèque de l'Arsenal, Paris.

Mary Homrighous, *The Grand Guignol* (unpublished dissertation, Northwestern University, 1963).

Paris Plaisirs (Paris) #102 December 1930.

Francois Rivière and Gabrielle Wittkop, *Grand Guignol* (Paris, 1979).

P.E. Schneider, "Fading Horrors of the Grand Guignol," *The New York Times Magazine*, March 17th, 1957.

F. Berkeley Smith, *How Paris Amuses Itself* (NY and London, 1903).

Le Théâtre (Paris) 1969, Number 2. Grand Guignol Issue, edited by Arrabal.

ONE HUNDRED PLOTS FROM THE REPERTOIRE OF THE GRAND GUIGNOL

LTHOUGH SOME FRENCH HISTORIANS have claimed that there were between 4,000 and 7,000 scripts written for the Theatre of the Grand Guignol of Paris and its short-lived competitors between 1897 and 1962, those figures are not only extraordinarily overstated but arithmetically impossible if they are referring to produced performances. The majority were, most likely, "accepted" into the repertoire but not staged. The number of produced plays is much closer to 1200 different dramas and sketches, of which one-third were frequently re-staged over several seasons. Some eighty or ninety appeared in print, either individually in contemporary journals and limited edition volumes or in play collections.

What follows are synopses of one-hundred of the most popular, or frequently performed, plays of the Grand Guignol—or approximately one-tenth of the entire sixty-five year repertoire. My source material derives from the published scripts, accounts of spectators and journalists, descriptions in the Grand Guignol programs and press releases, and various literary analyses, including M. E. Homrighous's *The Grand Guignol*. (It should be noted that the descriptions in the programs and playbills were occasionally inaccurate.)

A typical evening of the Grand Guignol normally fell into the simple alternating dramatic divisions of three comedies (and farces) and three horror plays (or psychological dramas). The patented whiplash effect of laughter and tears was known as "hot and cold showers." For this listing, I have divided the plots into three categories: Horror Plays, Comedies and Farces, and Dramatic Plays. Within each section, I have attempted to characterize the overriding themes, or emotional play, of the texts.

The themes of the Horror Plays have been separated into the following subsections: Helplessness, Infanticide, Insanity, Mutilation, Mysterious Death, Suffering of the Innocent, Suicide, Surgery, and Vengeance. The categories of the Comedies and Farces are Bourgeois Morality, Cuckoldry, Sex Farce, and Suffering of the Innocent. The Dramatic plots are divided into three categories: "Crass" Manners, Guilt, and Injustice.

In addition, six subsidiary themes are noted in the one-hundred synopses: Exoticism, Hypnosis, Imprisonment, Parisian Lowlife, Play-Transforming-Into-Terror, and Prostitution.

Certainly, the plots of many Grand Guignol plays—especially those written by André de Lorde—contain more than one theme, for instance: Helplessness, Insanity, Surgery, and Vengeance. Yet the horror (or humor) felt by the audience was normally predicated on a single overriding fear or emotion. While the overlapping and related themes make some plays difficult to affix to any one definitive group, I have attempted to place them in the category that best reveals their subliminal efficacy as a theatrical vehicle rather than a literary product. Included in the synopses are the authors' names and the date of the first performance of the play. Unless noted, the plays and sketches take place in one scene or act.

HORROR PLAYS

HELPLESSNESS

At the Telephone (André de Lorde and Charles Foley, 1902). *A two-act play, which was one of the best-known dramas of the Grand Guignol, with the additional themes of Imprisonment and the Suffering of the Innocent. It was first presented at the Theatre Antoine.*

André Marex, a prosperous Parisian businessman, has rented a backwoods country home for his wife, six-year old son, and his two elderly servants, Nanette and Blaise. Its unwholesome rustic quality and isolation are a great irritation for Marex. Only the newly installed telephone allows him to communicate with the outside world. In order to arrive in Paris the next day, Marex is forced to leave for a distant neighbor's house in the midst of a storm. To calm Martha, his wife, he shows her where his pistol is located. After Marex departs, a tramp visits the house and clandestinely pockets the pistol. Blaise, the old man servant, is notified that his ancient mother is ill. Martha persuades him to go immediately to her sick bed.

Later after dinner at his friends' home, Marex receives several telephone calls from Martha. She is frightened by the noises outside the country house. Each time, Marex attempts to allay her fears. Finally, when Martha calls, Marex realizes that intruders are breaking into the house. He listens in helpless agitation as members of his family are strangled.

The Land of Fright (André de Lorde and Eugene Morel, 1907). *A horror play in three acts with the additional themes of Exoticism and Imprisonment. Based on an actual incident in 1902, this play was first performed at the Theatre Antoine.*

In an underground penal colony in Martinique, French prisoners hear rumblings above the earth. They soon realize that a huge volcano has erupted. Trapped below the ground and abandoned, the prisoners panic. One claims that they are in the safest place. Another predicts that the fumes from the lava will soon consume their supply of oxygen. Slowly the sulphurous clouds suffocate the prisoners.

The Workshop for the Blind (Lucien Descaves, 1911). *A horror play with the additional theme of Imprisonment.*

A group of six blind men toil in a public workhouse making brushes. Each expresses his individual feeling about his daily condition: one is grateful to have a roof over his head; another feels that they are being exploited; still another preaches rebellion and revenge against their benefactors. When the blind men threaten the foreman with their knives, he locks them in the room and runs for the police. Outside their room the winter winds howl and the stove makes a roaring sound. Now in their solitude and separation from the outside world except for the strange noises by the window, the blind men are thrown, little by little, into a state of panic. The wind and sounds of the water pump make the blind men suddenly imagine that their building is on fire. They try to break down the door. A fight ensues and they attack each other with the knives. One throws himself out of the window.

In the Face of Death (Alfred Savoir and Léopold Marchand, 1920). *A three-act horror play with the additional themes of Cuckoldry, Guilt, Imprisonment, Mysterious Death, and Vengeance.*

In an outpost of a small colonial settlement in French Equatorial Africa, Christian, a French hunter in his thirties, hears three gunshots. His African servant, Gildas, has been ordered by Dr. Plassant to kill all dogs, including his own, to curtail an outbreak of rabies. Eve, the doctor's wife, runs through the jungle to be with her lover, Christian. She complains that they are so isolated from civilization that no one can be cured in time to prevent a maddening death by the highly-contagious rabies. They declare their love for one another. Dr. Plassant appears at Christian's door and Eve hides in another room of the cabin. The elderly physician discusses his sexual and family problems with Christian. Both Plassants have inadvertently mentioned to Christian that they have decided to keep one small dog in their house. The doctor departs. Christian attempts to bring the lascivious Eve home to her husband but as night falls she seduces him in his cabin. Silently, Dr. Plassant enters Christian's bedroom. Finding his wife asleep in Christian's arms, Dr. Plassant prepares two syringes and jabs the needles into an arm of each lover. He locks the doors and windows of the cabin. When the couple awakens, the doctor tells them that while they slept he injected one of them with a dose of the African disease.

The lovers are locked in the room with a sharp knife for protection. Each of them believes that the other is contaminated from the injection. In their hysteria, accusations fly back and forth. Finally, Eve runs madly toward Christian, who stabs her in a moment of self-preservation.

After his wife dies, Dr. Plassant enters. He accuses Christian of murder. The serum he injected in both of them was a harmless solution. Christian has killed a harmless woman. To prove his case, Dr. Plassant kisses his wife before Gildas—shouting from the outside—can warn him. Eve, in fact, contracted rabies from her dog. Now her husband has the disease. The doctor runs out. Christian discovers that he has cut his hand on the knife during his struggle with Eve. He, too, will die from the epidemic.

The Grip of Death, or the Hands of Hardouin (Jean Sartène, 1922). *One of the most frequently produced horror plays—it played some 1,000 times by 1933 and was translated into most European languages as well as Japanese. The play contains the additional themes of Cuckoldry and Vengeance.*

The Hardouins are a family of successful wine-growers in Burgundy. Now 80 years old, speechless, totally paralyzed, and confined to a wheelchair, the patriarch Jean-Marie was once a vigorous worker with amazingly strong hands. His son, Hippolyte, a man of 50, has married Rose, a woman of 24, against Jean-Marie's will. With her young lover, Etienne, Rose plans to take over the Hardouins' property. Jean-Marie witnesses Rose's treachery, which she flaunts before him, but is powerless to tell his son about it. While Hippolyte is away, one of his workmen almost falls to his death on the rotten stairs to the two-story-deep cellar. The son returns and starts down the same stairs for a bottle of wine. The father, speechless from paralysis, looks on but cannot warn him. At first, Rose says nothing and Hippolyte starts down to a certain death. Just as he falls down the stairwell, Rose screams and kneels beside the old paralyzed man. Suddenly Jean-Marie regains

control of his muscles and strangles her with his celebrated hands.

The Blind Ship (Max Maurey, 1927). *A horror play that closely resembles Maurice Maeterlinck's 1890 Symbolist masterpiece,* The Blind. *It contains the additional themes of Imprisonment and Insanity.*

The entire crew of a freighter, sailing in the vast ocean, is struck blind in a flash epidemic. When a steamer is heard in the distance, the sightless sailors desperately flash SOS signals. The steamer ignores them and the ship continues out into the endless and empty waters.

No Orchids for Miss Blandish (Marcel Duhamel, 1950). *This was a full-length, two-hour production adapted from the British mystery novel by Rene Raymond. Also with the additional themes of Exoticism, Imprisonment, Suffering of the Innocent and Vengeance.*

The psychotic American gangster, Slim Grisson, kidnaps the blonde Miss Blandish and holds her hostage. During her incarceration, where she is tied down in her bra and panties, she is sexually threatened by the drooling Grisson. Old Ma Grisson, the boss of the gang, beats Miss Blandish with a rubber hose so that she will silently submit to her son's pleasure. Both Grissons are finally killed in a police shoot out.

INFANTICIDE

The Final Torture (André de Lorde and Eugene Morel, 1904). *A celebrated horror play with the additional themes of Exoticism, Guilt, Helplessness, Imprisonment, Insanity, and Mutilation.*

During the 1900 Boxer Rebellion in China, the French consulate outside Peking has been surrounded for thirty-two days. Appeals to France have brought no response. Several Frenchmen in the isolated building have attempted to escape but without success. One heroic marine, Bornin, returns to the consulate with his hands cut off as evidence that the Chinese will show no mercy. Showing his bloody stumps, Bornin describes the atrocities that the other captured Europeans have suffered, then dies. The head consul D'Hemelin, realizing what will happen to his daughter, Denise, when the Chinese overrun the consulate, asks his subordinate, Georges Gravier, to kill her. In love with the daughter, Gravier refuses, forcing D'Hemelin to shoot his own daughter to prevent her torture. At this tragic moment, the Allied army arrives. A bugle sounds, the consulate is saved. D'Hemelin becomes insane.

The Obsession (André de Lorde and Alfred Binet, 1905). *A two-act horror play with the additional theme of Insanity.*

Jean is cursed with the obsession to kill his young son, Pierre. A famous Parisian psychologist explains to Jean that he is the victim of a progressive and incurable hereditary disease. Within a short period of time, Jean will be totally insane and unable to curb his murderous impulse. The psychologist advises that Jean commit himself to a mental asylum immediately. Jean, however, refuses to do so and returns home.

He confesses to his wife that he, not his daughter, accidently hit Pierre the other day. She thinks little of it and sends him into Pierre's room to apologize and bid the boy goodnight. In the room Jean strangles his son.

Sabotage (Charles Hellen, W. Valcros, Pol d'Estoc, 1910). *A horror play with the additional themes of Guilt and Surgery.*

Called to the house of a sick child in a working-class district, Dr. Margy quickly realizes that only immediate surgery can save the girl's life. Using a neighbor as a nurse, Margy performs a make-shift emergency operation. Everything looks successful, except suddenly the electric lights go out. After a long search for a candle and matches, the child's mother, Angele, finally lights the candle's wick. Now Margy informs her of the bad news: her little girl expired during the dark lull. A door opens. Returning from a union demonstration against the local power station, the child's father enters the room triumphantly. While his fellow workers sing the "Internationale" outside the family's house, the father explains that it was his idea to cut the electricity in the district as a way of showing the bosses the workers' strength. Angele grabs him by the throat and calls her husband a murderer.

The Keepers of the Lighthouse (Paul Autier and Paul Cloquemin, 1918). *One of the most popular horror plays with the additional themes of Guilt, Insanity, and Imprisonment.*

A father and son are the keepers of a lighthouse off the coast of Brittany. It is winter and they are completely shut off from the world for two months. A terrible storm is raging. Waves are beating against the lighthouse. The son tells a story of how one lighthouse keeper died at the beginning of his duty and his partner was forced to stay with the corpse for the whole two months. A few days earlier, the son confesses, he was bitten by a dog which may have had rabies. Suddenly, the son is seized with

hydrophobia and insanity. He realizes that he is doomed to die in a most painful fashion. He begs his father to kill him. The thirst and madness worsen. Then the young man, foaming at the mouth, attacks his father and the father is torn between saving his son and signalling a chartless ship, which will soon dash against the rocks. He strangles his son and just manages to switch on the beacon of light, which saves the lives of the sailors on the boat.

The Dead Child (André de Lorde, 1918). *A three-act horror play with the additional themes of Cuckoldry, Insanity, Mutilation, and Vengeance.*

A celebrated sculptor, Le Hirec returns home from abroad. He discovers that his wife has left him for another man. She has also abandoned their ill baby, who has since died.

Le Hirec becomes insane from grief. Taking the boy's bones, nails, and hair from his grave, Le Hirec fashions a wax mannequin of his son.

Sometime later, Le Hirec's wife returns to him in remorse. Her initial happiness turns to disgust when Le Hirec shows her his effigy-child. She attempts to escape when he forces her to hold the wax model. Le Hirec has locked the doors. She runs upstairs to the child's room. Le Hirec follows her inside and strangles her, reappearing to murmur that she will never leave him again.

Rapid 13 (Jean Sartène, 1921). *A horror play with the additional themes of Guilt and Helplessness.*

An embittered switchman of the railroad company decides to wreck one of the newest trains, the Rapid 13, when it passes his station by not pulling the proper lever. In

the control room with his daughter, the switchman is reminded at the last minute that his granddaughter is on the on-coming Rapid 13. He suffers a paralyzing heart attack and cannot grip the necessary switch. Responding to his gestures and nods, the railman's daughter throws a switch, but it is the wrong one. As the two hold each other in desperation, the Rapid 13 hurls into still another train, undoubtedly killing the switchman's granddaughter, his daughter's daughter.

INSANITY

The System of Dr. Goudron and Prof. Plume (André de Lorde, 1903). *One of the most celebrated horror plays, this was adapted from Edgar Allan Poe's 1845 short story* The System of Dr. Tarr and Professor Fether. *With the additional theme of Mutilation.*

Two journalists, Henri and Jean, visit the office of Dr. Goudron, who is said to have pioneered a humane treatment to cure insanity. As the doctor begins to describe his system, the reporters hear cries and pounding from an adjoining room. Goudron investigates. Another scream is heard and Goudron laughs. The reporters begin to suspect that the doctor himself may be mad. Finally when he parades his colleagues and assistants, who start to behave in an odd manner and then to imitate animals, Henri and Jean realize that they are the ones in danger. A storm increases the mad assistants' insanity. Henri and Jean discover that the insane patients have taken over the asylum and are playing the roles of the attendants. The institution's guards rescue the journalists at the last minute, fighting off the murderous inmates. In the doctor's

closet, the real Goudron has been murdered and mutilated. The guards drag out his butchered body as the inmates shriek and laugh in the distance.

A Concert at the Madhouse (André de Lorde and Charles Foley, 1909). *A horror play in two acts.*

At an insane asylum run by a cynical and neurotic director, various inmates exhibit their bizarre and comical personas. One thinks that she is made of porceline. Another imagines that he is a railroad. Still another writes modern poetry. An old woman, declared cured, is taken home by her son.

That same evening, however, she returns to the institution, disgusted by her daughter-in-law and grandson's unwelcome reception. Suddenly one of the insane rushes the complaining woman and strangles her to death.

The Mysterious Man (André de Lorde, 1921). *A three-act horror play with the additional theme of the Suffering of the Innocent.*

The head of a successful engineering firm, Raymound Bercier, has suddenly become afflicted with severe and violent episodes of paranoia. His wife, whom he has attempted to strangle, and Bercier's physician have him institutionalized.

Not knowing about the murderous struggle with his wife, Bercier's brother, a co-founder of the business, persuades the family, including his sister-in-law, to sign a petition for Bercier's release. Bercier cunningly pretends to be cured when brought before a magistrate. The head psychologist of the asylum claims that Bercier is so dangerous that he should never be released. When asked to prove his assertion, the psychologist is constantly interrupted by Bercier's brother, which prevents Bercier's madness from being revealed. The judge declares Bercier sane.

Later that day, Bercier returns home and quickly slashes his wife with a knife and strangles his brother to death.

The Cabinet of Caligari (André de Lorde and Henri Bauche, 1925). *A popular horror play in seven (later nine) scenes, this was based on the dream-like 1919 German Expressionist film classic. It contains the additional themes of Hypnosis and Mysterious Death.*

Alain and Francis plan to break out of an asylum to find Dr. Caligari, a carnival hypnotist, who Francis believes can restore their sanity. As they escape from the madhouse, the apparition of the murdered Jeanne, Francis' fiancee, appears. Francis suddenly declares that Caligari killed her as he does to all the beautiful and young people. Later, before Caligari's circus tent, Jeanne volunteers to be hypnotized by Caligari. Francis, knowing of her weak heart, asks to replace her. Under hypnosis, Francis reveals that Jeanne will die before dawn. Alain tries to get Caligari to awaken Francis, who is led into Caligari's stall. That night, the startled Jeanne cannot sleep. From her window, the somnambulant Francis reaches in and carries her away. Meanwhile the police investigate Caligari's booth. He shows them a wax effigy of Francis, which they believe is the hypnotized Francis. After they leave, the real Francis brings in Jeanne. When Caligari embraces her, she calls out and dies. Francis is then instructed to bury her in a cemetery, where Caligari awakens Francis. Later, Francis and Alain are back in the asylum courtyard. Francis convinces the inmates that the head of the institution is really Caligari. Francis is put into a straight jacket and tossed into a padded cell. There he sees Caligari at the window making a strangling gesture. Francis dies.

The Eyes of the Ghost (Jean Aragny, 1926). *A horror play with the additional themes of Guilt, Imprisonment, and Vengeance.*

The chief of a hospital for the mentally ill, Doctor Tardier, a humane physician and gentle person, is concerned for the safety of his patients. One of his inmates has been murdered the previous night at midnight. Tardier increases the number of guards and reprimands one of them for his brutality to the mentally ill. At midnight, another patient is murdered. The patients discover that the murderer is the sleepwalking Doctor Tardier himself. As a storm rages outside, the doctor's patients gouge out his eyes.

The Naked Man (Charles Méré, 1928). *A three-act horror play.*

In an old chateau, a woman has lost her sanity since she gave birth to a half-human monster. Her husband keeps their humanoid son chained up in a cage but has managed to teach him basic ideas of obedience and respect. The mother and a friend release the monster, who unexpectedly attacks the woman and is shot and killed by the friend. Finding his son dead, the father goes insane.

MUTILATION

The Little House in Auteuil (Robert Scheffer and Georges Liguereux, 1907). *A horror play with the additional themes of Prostitution and Vengeance.*

At a small brothel, there is a prostitute who enjoys watching people in pain and suffering. She welcomes a man who soon confesses that he was an accomplice in a murder. The prostitute demands that he describe it and then re-enact the killing with her as the murdered victim so she may enjoy the thrill of terror. The criminal too becomes a kind of victim in the story and has himself tied up. Another sadist, a client of the prostitute, arrives unexpectedly in the room. Seeing the criminal bound to a chair, the sadist rips out his beard, pulls his teeth and nails out, cuts open the man's face with a knife, and burns out his eyes. While the victim screams in agony, the tormentor becomes sexually excited by the sight of blood and savagely possesses the prostitute.

Hsioung-Pe-Ling, or the Bloody Aloutte (Charles Garin, 1911). *A "Chinese" horror play in two scenes with the additional themes of Exoticism and Vengeance.*

In ancient China, Hsioung-Pe-Ling has been entrusted with her husband's beautiful and superbly trained aloutte while he is away. Master Ling has been called to the emperor's side just at the time of a regional contest, in which his bird would have won first prize. His jealous neighbor, whose bird is second only to Ling's, takes advantage of Ling's absence. He visits Hsioung-Pe and convinces her to show him the aloutte. Promising to teach her the commands needed to control the bird, the neighbor tricks Hsioung-Pe into opening the cage, which allows the bird to fly away. When Ling returns, Hsioung-Pe tells him an obvious lie that someone stole the aloutte.

Ling then invites the neighbor over for a visit. Through clever and suspenseful conversation, Ling confirms his suspicions. He terrifies and then kills the man in front of Hsioung-Pe's parents, who are present as witnesses. "But where is our daughter? Where is she?" they ask of Ling. Ling then lifts the cover of the bird cage to reveal his wife's severed head, her punishment for disloyalty.

The Mark of the Beast (E.M. Laumann, 1916). *An adaptation from Rudyard Kipling's short story, this horror play in two acts contains the additional themes of Exoticism, Mysterious Death, and Vengeance.*

After a drunken New Year's Eve party in a British fort in Northern India, three Englishmen arrive at the Temple of Hanuman, the monkey god. While the Hindu priests chant their morning prayers, the thoroughly-inebriated financier, Fleete, grinds the end of his cigar into the forehead of the red monkey idol. While his friends unsuccessfully attempt to pull him away, Fleete shouts that he has made "the mark of the beast" on the shrine. Meanwhile, amidst the uproar of the local priests, the Silver Man, a naked leper, appears and drops over Fleete, burrowing his flesh-eaten face into Fleete's breast. Suddenly, the priests become calm and one of their leaders tells the Englishmen to leave quickly. Sobering up, Fleete complains about a sharp smell of human blood, which the others cannot detect.

At the house of Commissioner Strickland, one of the three Britishers, Fleete awakens the next morning with a great hunger for uncooked meat. Strickland notices a strange set of black markings on Fleete's chest. During the day, Fleete acts more and more mad, scaring the horses and rolling in the ground, finally turning into a wolf-like animal. Fleete's friends bind him as the Silver Man mews from outside the house. Dr. Dumoise inspects Fleete and announces that he is dying from an advanced case of rabies. The physician departs. Within minutes, Strickland captures the Silver Man as he dances with his shadow in the moonlight. The Englishmen torture him with ropes and a white-hot branding iron. Eventually, the exhausted leper agrees to cure Fleete, which he does by placing his hand on Fleete's breast and inhaling. Fleete opens his eyes now cured. The Silver Man is released. Dumoise re-enters with a death certificate. He is shocked to see a living Fleete. Fleete sniffs and complains about the "doggy smell" (really, singed flesh) in the room.

The Man of the Night (André de Lorde and Léo Marchès, 1921). *A horror play.*

An artist has developed an obsession with the dead. He finds immense pleasure in digging up corpses and disfiguring them. Their lifeless bodies become the secret of his realistic paintings.

The Garden of Torture (Pierre Chaine, 1922). *An adaptation from Octave Mirbeau's decadent novel, this popular three-act horror play contains additional themes of Exoticism, Imprisonment, and Vengeance.*

On a French ship to Shanghai, a Chinese man makes advances to Clara Watson, a married English woman. Marchal, a French army officer and the woman's lover, throws the Chinese overboard, drowning him.

At the luxurious residence of the Watsons on the Chinese mainland, Clara persuades Marchal to desert the army to live with her. Secretly in league with the Chinese rebels, Clara attempts to use her position to protect Marchal when they kidnap him. The lovers discover that the Chinese man who Marchal tossed into the ocean was an important figure in the underground movement.

Both Marchal and Clara are brought to the infamous Garden of Torture, where traitors and enemies of the rebels are punished with bizarre and exotic tortures. They see strips of flesh ripped from a young woman's back. The other prisoners describe in obsessive detail the forms of punishment and mutilation that are practiced in the Garden of Torture. Marchal and Clara are tortured and killed. Clara's eyes are pierced with red-hot needles before her execution.

A Crime in the Madhouse (André de Lorde and Alfred Binet, 1925). *This perennially popular two-act horror play was later retitled* The Infernals, *or* The Old Women. *It contains the additional themes of Helplessness, Imprisonment, Insanity, and the Suffering of the Innocent.*

In a lunatic asylum, a beautiful girl, Louise, pleads with the head psychiatrist to release her immediately since she has been declared cured. Thinking that she is showing new signs of hysteria, he orders her confined for another night.

In Louise's cell are two hideous mad women, Hunchback and the Normandy Woman. To assuage Louise's fear of them, an unsympathetic Sister is assigned to stand watch through the night. The Sister, however, quickly vacates the cell to attend a funeral service in the asylum chapel. Ignoring Louise's desperate entreaties to stay, the Sister maintains that Louise's morbid premonitions are a product of her hysteria and departs. Suddenly, One-Eye, a madwoman so violent that she is kept in solitary, enters Louise's cell. The old crones believe that a cuckoo bird is imprisoned behind Louise's eyes.

THÉÂTRE DU
GRAND GUIGNOL

LE JARDIN DES SUPPLICES

LE JARDIN DES
SUPPLICES

DRAME en 3 tableaux de M. P. Chaine d'après le Célèbre Roman
d'Octave MIRLEAU

*"Suddenly an apparition of
Joubert's drowned wife appears."*
—from A Kiss of Blood

While the first two women pin down Louise's arms, One-Eye gouges out her eyes with a knitting needle. Now fearful of what they have done, one of the insane women pushes One-Eye's face against a hot plate that was just used to boil water. The old woman's face is totally destroyed in smoke and flame. It is reduced to an oozing mass of charred and bloody flesh.

The Kiss of Blood (Jean Aragny and Francis Neilson, 1929). *A horror play in two acts with the additional themes of Guilt, Insanity, Mysterious Death, Surgery, and Vengeance.*

Joubert asks his friend Dr. Leduc to amputate one of his fingers, which is causing him horrific pain. Since there is no wound or infection, Leduc pretends to perform the operation, giving Joubert a simple sedative. When Joubert awakes, the pain in his finger is more intense still. He unwinds the surgical gauze and discovers the doctor's trick. Taking a scalpel, Joubert proceeds to amputate his own finger.

The next day in Joubert's apartment, Dr. Leduc visits him. Suddenly an apparition of Joubert's drowned wife appears, and she kisses Joubert's bandaged hand. The intense pain reappears and the agitated Joubert drops dead. The startled doctor finds out that the ghost was no psychic vision. The real Madame Joubert, now laughing madly at her husband's psychosomatic death, is an escapee from an insane asylum. Previously, Joubert thought that he had murdered his wife by throwing her overboard from a cruise ship. Unbeknownst to him, the woman was rescued by sailors but lost her mind as a result of the murder attempt. They placed her in an institution, from which she escaped.

The Bloody Trunk (Maurice Level, 1931). *A controversial two-act horror play.*

Two penniless students lose all their money—borrowed money—in a poker game. They then kill the young and beautiful Mlle. Soller in order to steal her purse, which is filled with bank notes. They chop up and hide her body in an empty travel trunk.

Just as they start to flee, a creditor comes to reclaim Soller's furniture, including the bloody chest-suitcase. Terrified of being discovered, one of the killers confesses immediately. The second student, furious at his friend's cowardice, shoots him in the head.

Orgy in the Lighthouse (Léopold Marchand, 1956). *A frequently produced horror play with the additional themes of Insanity, Play Transforming Into Terror, and Prostitution.*

In a lighthouse off the Breton coast, an elderly marine attendant, Logonadee, and his young assistant, Yann, watch a religious procession taking place across the water during a feast day. A sailor on leave, Yves, Yann's wild brother, unexpectedly appears in the tower with bottles of calavados for the alcoholic Logonadee, and two prostitutes, Rosa and Nini, for his entertainment and that of his somewhat inexperienced brother. While Logonadee proceeds to get drunk, the brothers dance with the whores and become playful. Rosa, the more sexually aggressive of the women, enjoys roughhouse games. Nini reveals that Rosa insulted the priest at the festival earlier in the day. She also offends the respectful Yann by comparing his statue of the Virgin with her whorehouse madame. As an intense storm appears on the horizon, Logonadee retires to the top of the lighthouse with his calavados. In the

"Sol Hyams refuses to sell the diamond."
—*from* Sol Hyams, the Pawnbroker

darkness of the tower, the couples participate in a sexual orgy, which concludes in a drunken slumber. A siren call from a lost boat awakens Yves. The light beacon has gone out and a boat containing the sailors' mother is approaching the treacherous rocks below. Logonadee has locked the door to the beacon, and Yann becomes hysterical, blaming his predicament on the blasphemy of the prostitutes. Yves discovers that one of the women stole the statue of the Virgin. Declaring her the devil, he cuts Rosa's throat and throws her from the window of the lighthouse. The boat with the men's mother crashes against the rocks. In a religious frenzy, the sailors decide to burn Nini to death. After pouring gasoline on her, they incinerate her and pray.

MYSTERIOUS DEATH

Sol Hyams, the Pawnbroker (Jean Bernac, 1907). *A two-act dramatization of the mystery story by the British writer, W.W. Jacobs. It contains the additional themes of Exoticism, Guilt, and Vengeance.*

Three men have stolen a precious diamond in India. The first thief betrayed his partners and ran off with the gem. After a long pursuit and capture, the other two thieves killed the first and retained his booty. Then the second thief stole the diamond in turn from the third, a Hindu, and escaped to London. In the pawnshop of Sol Hyams, the second thief sells the diamond. Just outside the shop, he is murdered by his Hindu partner.

The Indian then enters Hyams' establishment and attempts to purchase the diamond for Hyams' original price. Hyams refuses to sell it. After much haggling, the Hindu departs, predicting a horrible death for Hyams. As foretold, Hyams dies at the appointed hour in a mysterious and terrifying manner.

The Man Who Saw the Devil (Gaston Leroux, 1911). *A two-act horror play with the additional theme of Guilt by the author of the novel* The Phantom of the Opera.

In the midst of the Juas mountains, four tourists find an abandoned manor. The owner of the dilapidated castle has sold his soul to the devil in exchange for the power to always win at cards. The devil appeared to the old man in a mirror hung on the inside of a closet. The secret lover of one of the female tourists opens the fatal wardrobe and asks the devil for the death of the woman's husband. He then breaks the mirror and faints.

The next day, he aims an unloaded gun at the husband and pretends to fire. The husband drops dead.

The Siege of Berlin (Charles Hellen and Pol d'Estoc, 1914). *A horror play with the additional theme of Bourgeois Morality.*

In the relic-ladden apartment of the eighty-year-old Colonel Jouve, a veteran of the Napoleonic wars, the ancient warrior and his twenty-year-old granddaughter, Helene, await the parade of the victors of the Franco-Prussian war of 1870-1. Fearing for his pride and sanity, Helene—along with Doctor Valbert and friends of the colonel—has informed her grandfather over the last two years of fighting that the seemingly invincible French Army has conquered the Germans, its natural enemy. In fact, the opposite is true, and when the military parade comes close to the apartment, the granddaughter cannot constrain the old

LE CHÂTEAU
DE LA
MORT LENTE

man from cheering his heroes. Then at the window, the colonel realizes that it is the Prussian Army, not the French, who are marching through Paris. The old colonel becomes totally insane for a moment, stiffens, then dies at the feet of his granddaughter.

Crucified, or the Night of the Twelfth of May, 1848 (A.P. Antoine and Charles Poidlouse, 1923). *A two-act horror play with the additional themes of Exoticism, Guilt, and Vengeance.*

William Stone, an Irish patriot, lives with his daughter Ellen and son Billy on Lord Kindlard's farm. Larkin and his son Jack, though Irish, are loyal British subjects. Three years ago in 1845, Jack Larkin called on Ellen and saw three revolutionaries paying Stone a visit. They informed Stone that his son Billy had been captured and crucified. The Irishmen detected Larkin listening to their conversation and crucified him on the door of the cottage.

On each anniversary of Jack's death, one of the four murderers has been killed in a supernatural way. Only old Stone is left. It is the anniversary night. Stone and a friend are about to flee when revenge enters.

Gott Mit Uns (René Berton, 1928). *A horror play with the themes of Guilt, Imprisonment, and Mutilation. On its first revival in 1929, it was re-titled The Light in the Tomb and given an internationalist finale with the German spy praising France as he dies.*

During a First World War engagement, a group of French soldiers take control of a cave from a fleeing German army. As soon as the French unit enters, a German shell hits the mouth of the cave, which thoroughly traps them inside. The French then discover a lone German soldier, Hermann, left behind to spy on the advancing French. Hermann, however, was trying to dig his way out of the cave since a ticking time bomb was secreted inside. Now Hermann, as a martyr for his homeland, refuses to reveal where the explosive is located. The French soldiers threaten him with physical violence and torture, but Hermann will not yield. The French captain, formerly a professor of philosophy like Hermann, finally persuades him to disclose the bomb's whereabouts. It is defused just seconds before it was about to be activated. Meanwhile, an engineering unit of the French Army has tunneled through the blocked entrance of the cave and rescues the trapped soldiers. Hermann runs outside and is hit by a German shell. He returns to the cave with his face blown away. Now once again a loyal German, Hermann shouts, "Gott mit uns!" ("God is with us!") and dies.

SUFFERING OF THE INNOCENT

The Castle of Slow Death (André de Lorde and Henri Bauche, 1916). *A horror play with the themes of Exoticism, Helplessness, Imprisonment, and Vengeance.*

In a luxurious retreat in the Rocky Mountains, where everyone is dressed in cowboy attire, a thief breaks into a wealthy woman's room. She fights to keep the diamond necklace that she is wearing. The thief strangles her, takes all her jewels and flees. He is stopped, however, by the guards of the asylum. The thief has entered a leprosarium and most likely contracted a highly contagious form of leprosy. In the background, one can hear the mysterious chanting of funeral processions. Now the thief himself must be confined to the resort as both prisoner and patient.

The Night of Terror (Charles Méré, 1919). *One of the most successful horror plays with the additional themes of Imprisonment, Parisian Low-life, and Play Transforming Into Terror, and Suffering of the Innocent.*

Italian Prince Atalonga wagers the Duchesse de Martigny that she will not accompany him to a resort frequented by cut-throats. Together they visit a room in the Cafe Bonnardel, where he plays a practical joke on her, making her believe that he is an *apache* attempting to rob her. Atalonga believes this will give the Duchesse a special thrill. Suddenly real *apaches* storm the room and the prince attempts to explain his joke. But, as the *apaches* break down the door, the Duchesse panics and stabs the prince to death. Thinking that she is a thief like them, the *apaches* hail the Duchesse. After taking the prince's money and jewels, they throw his corpse out the window and thank her, leaving her alone in the room.

The Three Masks (Charles Méré, 1922). *A horror play with the additional themes of Exoticism and Vengeance.*

A young Corsican, Paolo Della Corba, is in love with Viola, the daughter of a family that has sworn a vendetta against Paolo's family. Paolo's father, a proud and strict army colonel, refuses to allow the two to marry, even though Viola is now carrying Paolo's baby. His father decides to send him to join the army in France, which will separate the two lovers and keep him safe from Viola's three murderous brothers.

It is Carnival time and, believing that Viola's brothers are out of town, the two lovers make secret plans to put on Carnival costumes and enjoy their last night together. Later that evening, three masked revellers appear at the Della Corba house, dragging a fourth with them who is dressed as a Pierrot. Paolo's father drinks and celebrates with them. The three celebrants apologize for their "drunken companion," who has not moved from the chair he was placed in. The three men depart, leaving the fourth in the chair. Then Viola comes into the house, frantically looking for Paolo whom she says is dressed as a Pierrot. The father lifts the mask of the man in the chair with trepidation and finds Paolo's bloody, lifeless face underneath.

The Cell 13 (Roland Dreyfus, 1926). *A horror play with the additional theme of Imprisonment.*

A man has been convicted and imprisoned, although completely innocent of his accused crime. He attempts an escape but is surprised by a prison guard and kills him in self-defense. Just then the prison director arrives to tell the unjustly convicted man that he will be released. A man has confessed to the crime for which he was imprisoned. Now, however, the innocent man is truly a murderer. He will remain in Cell 13 forever.

The Merchant of Corpses (André de Lorde, 1940). *A horror play in two acts with the additional theme of Guilt.*

A mother anxiously awaits her daughter who is late from school. She has heard about a child-murderer who always reappears at carnival time. In the distance is the growing sound of the music from a street carnival. When her child fails to return home, the mother denounces a carnival employee as

TOURNÉE DU THÉÂTRE
DU
GRAND GUIGNOL
DE PARIS C.CHOISY Directeur
LES 3 MASQUES

DRAME
DE
M. Charles MÉRÉ

IMMENSE
SUCCÈS

the murderer of her daughter. Since there is no dead body, the police can do nothing.

A friend of the woman kidnaps the accused man and plunges him into a vat of acid that is used to prepare skeletons for a medical department. The mother faints when she sees the chemically deteriorating body. She passes out because the dead man was innocent; her daughter has already safely returned home.

SUICIDE

Night at the Hampton Club (André Mouëzy-Eon and Armont, 1908). *A horror play inspired by Robert Louis Stevenson's short story collection,* The Suicide Club. *It contains the additional themes of Helplessness, Imprisonment, and Play Transforming Into Terror.*

Herbert Forbes, a British journalist, has managed to gain entrance under false pretenses to the secretive Suicide Club. The sole purpose of the elite London society is to facilitate the suicides of its members. Forbes joins the other members at a card table. Whoever draws the death card that night must kill himself. From the stressful intensity of the game, one member suffers a fatal heart attack. The game continues and Forbes is dealt the card of death. He quickly explains his true intent — to gather information for a newspaper article on the Suicide Club, not to kill himself. The President of the Club is sympathetic to his predicament, but he cannot permit any infraction of the rules: Forbes must kill himself. Now panicked, Forbes draws a revolver on the men. They ignore it, however, and leave the room. Forbes is alone in the bolted suicide room. After undergoing a roller coaster of changing moods, Forbes

puts the pistol to his head and shoots himself. The President re-enters and the others carry Forbes' corpse out on a prepared stretcher.

The Prison for Children (André de Lorde and Pierre Chaine, 1910). *A social drama that details the cruelty of fathers who abandon their sons to sadistic keepers of children's reformatories. It contains the additional themes of Imprisonment and the Suffering of the Innocent.*

One group of brutalized victims breaks out of the reformatory-prison, and one by one are caught by the authorities. Backed into a farmhouse, the young hero Georges decides to hang himself rather than return to the school.

Hara Kiri (Jean Sartène and Pierre Day, 1919). *A horror play with the additional themes of Exoticism, Guilt, and Mutilation.*

In a Japanese opium den, Barriere initiates his friend Mainville into the pleasures of the Orient. In the darkly lighted room, Thi Nam prepares the opium pipes while Mara Paiva performs a mysterious and illusory dance. When the Europeans are completely under the drug's influence, Thi Nam rapes and kills Barriere's wife, who is also Mainville's mistress. But suddenly realizing the depravity of his crime, Thi Nam decides to commit suicide and plunges a long knife into his stomach. His blood spurts across the room and he falls. Mara Paiva once again begins her exotic dancing under the protection of veils and multicolored lights.

SURGERY

A Lesson at Salpétrière (André de Lorde, 1908). *A horror play in two acts with the themes* *of Hypnosis, Insanity, Mutilation, and Vengeance.*

At Salpétrière, a medical school within a mental asylum, doctors perform experiments to cure insanity. While the chief doctor, Professor Marbois, conducts his lecture, an intern, Nicolo, executes his instructions. A first patient is cut open. Then a second with a bandaged head and paralyzed arm, Claire Camu, is wheeled in. She maintains that her arm injury was the result of an experiment at Salpétrière. Marbois assures her that she is suffering from an hallucination. Nicolo is ordered to hypnotize her. Under hypnosis, Claire remembers that it was Nicolo who shocked her with electrical currents and destroyed her nerves. Grabbing a bottle of sulfuric acid, she hurls it into Nicolo's face, causing him to fall to the floor

in excruciating pain. Claire is dragged off by the orderlies while Marbois lectures on the antidotes to sulfuric acid.

The Horrible Experiment (André de Lorde and Alfred Binet, 1909). *A popular two-act terror play with the additional theme of Vengeance.*

In his laboratory at his country home, Doctor Charrier has discovered how to resurrect human life by electrically stimulating the hearts of corpses. Charrier explains to his illustrious pupil and future son-in-law, Dr. Demare, that he is jealous of him since the young man is able to marry his daughter Jeanne, whom he raised and adored. Before the young lovers leave on a motorbicycle for Jeanne's grandmothers's house, the daughter announces that the two of them will return sooner than expected since she has discovered a shortcut.

After Jeanne and Demare leave, a stranger in black, the public executioner, enters and explains to Charrier that there will be an execution and Charrier will be able to test his theory of electrical resurrection on the body of the corpse. To caution the delighted Charrier, however, the executioner tells him a story about a guillotined man whose headless body clutched him so fiercely that they had to break the dead man's fingers. The man in black exits and the telephone rings. Jeanne has been killed in an accident with the motorbike. When her body is carried into the laboratory during a storm, Charrier decides to resurrect her, using Jeanne's horrified fiancee, Demare, as an assistant. Charrier makes an incision over her heart and applies an electrode to it. Jeanne begins to hemorrhage. The electricity goes out for a moment. A green light burns faintly as a battery hums. Suddenly there are sounds in her throat. Charrier increases the voltage. His daughter starts to breathe, then her arms stiffen and raise up. Charrier goes to embrace Jeanne's corpse but she strangles him, despite Demare's efforts to loosen her grip.

The Laboratory of Hallucinations (André de Lorde and Henri Bauche, 1916). *Another popular three-act de Lorde horror play with the additional themes of Cuckoldry, Insanity, Mutilation, and Vengeance.*

Sonia, the wife of Doctor Gorlitz, a brutal scientist and head of a sinister health clinic in the country, decides to run off with Monsieur de Mora, one of the doctor's neighbors. She tells her husband that she and de Mora will spend the afternoon innocently with a group to explore a nearby Roman ruins.

While Gorlitz and his assistant engage in torturous experiments with a screaming and bound patient, de Mora is brought to Gorlitz' laboratory. De Mora's car overturned and his skull was fractured. In de Mora's pocket, Gorlitz finds Sonia's love letter to him. Madly jealous, Gorlitz decides to revenge himself by operating on de Mora, poking and snipping the lobes inside his brain, until de Mora slowly becomes permanently deranged. Gorlitz reveals his plan to Sonia. Soon her lover will deteriorate into a mindless idiot. Gorlitz even shows her de Mora's current dementia.

De Mora overhears Gorlitz' explanation and, in a burst of energy, straps Gorlitz to the operating table, and cuts open his skull, subjecting him to a fate that was intended for himself.

The Man Who Killed Death (René Berton, 1928). *A horror play with the additional themes of Guilt, Insanity, and Mutilation.*

Outside a prison courtyard, a celebrated medical scientist, Professor Fargus, prepares the equipment for an experiment to determine whether consciousness remains in a severed human head. A convict is executed by guillotine and his bloody head is rushed in by the prison guards. Fargus places the head on a medical table and attaches electrical annodes to simulate the heart and brain activity. Then he injects beef blood into the arteries. Life returns to the convict's head. The head's eyes and mouth move. The prosecuting attorney, still not free from doubt about the dead man's guilt or innocence, asks him whether or not he was guilty of the crime for which he was guillotined. The head slowly intones, "No!" Inside the room, the guilt-ridden attorney goes mad.

VENGEANCE

The Cargo Fraud (André de Lorde and Masson-Forestier, 1906). *A horror play in two acts.*

The owner of a cargo ship, *The Gladiator*, Le Hertel has knowingly overloaded its container compartments, which will cause the boat to sink. Le Hertel does this to collect a large insurance premium despite the fact that the husband of his god-daughter is *The Gladiator*'s captain.

When news of *The Gladiator*'s fate— especially the drowning of the crew— become known, relatives and neighbors of the crew storm Le Hertel's office. He attempts to calm them but only in vain. They throw him out of the window and his body smashes against the pavement below.

The Dead Rat, Room No. 6 (André de Lorde and Pierre Chaine, 1908). *Also called* A Pair of White Gloves *in the English-speaking world, this was one of de Lorde's most successful productions, playing on the West End and Broadway in 1912 and 1913. There seem to be two versions of this play: one, where the girl is the sister of a revolutionary; and another, where she is an agent of the Czar sent to kill the philandering general. A horror play with the additional themes of Exoticism and Prostitution.*

General Gregoroff, a former officer in the Czarist army, is now living a life of dissipation in Paris. He meets an attractive prostitute, Lea, in the Rue de la Paix and falls in love with her. She agrees to dine with him in a private room in the Rat Mort.

Unbeknownst to him, Lea is the sister of a revolutionary who has been tortured and put to death under the general's regime as governor of Moscow. During the dinner, as he attempts to undress Lea, the general becomes dazed from too much wine and brags of his cruelty, including the torture of Lea's brother. Just then Lea reveals who she is and strangles him with her white gloves as the general screams for help.

The Closed Door (Robert Francheville, 1910). *A horror play with the additional theme of Mysterious Death.*

A doctor's wife died from injuries resulting from a fall. Had her husband operated on her, she would have survived. Her death, however, allowed the doctor to marry a younger woman. Now the dead woman's ghost haunts the doctor's house and entices her replacement into the master bedroom. There, a huge antique mirror falls on the doctor's second wife. The doctor rushes in to save her but the mirror has trapped the young woman and she bleeds to death. The doctor, devastated, declares her dead. The door to the room mysteriously closes.

Hot Earth (Henri-René Lenormand, 1913). *A horror play with the additional themes of Exoticism, Guilt, and Mutilation.*

In a jungle clearing in French Equatorial Africa, an African native, Maelik, is being lashed on his bare back. A French visitor, Prefailles, realizes that Maelik is clearly innocent of any crime. The French commander, Rouge, maintains that this is white man's justice. Later Maelik's wife comes to the camp requesting medical help for her husband. The wife of one of Rouge's officers, Madame Le Cormier, goes to assist. A short

period after Le Cormier's exit, the Africans return with a large bloody box. It contains Madame Le Cormier's head. Prefailles becomes hysterical about the madness of it all. Rouge then reminds Prefailles that twenty years before he learned about "white man's justice" from Prefailles' behavior.

A Kiss in the Night (Maurice Level, 1913). A two-act horror play with the additional theme of Mutilation.

Henri decides to break with his lover, who retaliates by throwing vitriol in his face, disfiguring him terribly. The girl is arrested but promptly freed as Henri refuses to prosecute.

Although forsaken, the girl shows compassion, and visits Henri for a last time. He asks her to kiss him, and she is filled with revulsion as she looks at his scarred features. When their lips meet, Henri strangles her.

The Experiment of Dr. Lorde (Hasmyck and Wattyne, 1916). A horror play in three acts that exploited the name and characterization of André de Lorde. With the additional theme of the Suffering of the Innocent.

In the outskirts of Paris, Dr. Lorde has established a "psycholgical laboratory." There, he has created the means to transfer the soul of one body to that of another. The subjects of his experiment are a famous English strangler and a young scholar, who is betrothed to the daughter of Lorde's rival. Dr. Lorde transmits the soul (or mind) of the criminal to the young man.

The strangler-in-the-body-of-the-scholar reveals his true idenity and begins a series of heinous crimes, ending in the strangulation of his fiancee. Now, hunted by the police, the monster returns to the laboratory and kills Dr. Lorde.

The Mask (Jesse and H.M. Harwood, 1916). A horror play adapted from an English drama with the additional theme of Cuckoldry.

A victim of a mining accident, James Glasson has to wear a mask in order to shield others from the sight of his grotesquely disfigured face. He suspects his wife, Vashti, of being unfaithful and plots to catch her with her lover. Pretending to leave the house, Glasson secrets himself in the room where he quickly discovers Willie, his wife's lover. Glasson overhears that Vashti and Willie plan to run off together. When his wife leaves the room, Glasson attacks Willie, who murderously pushes Glasson to the floor. Vashti returns and, thinking that her husband has been killed, cold-bloodedly advises Willie to dispose of her husband's corpse in the old mine shaft. She even provides Willie with a mask for the perfect disguise as her husband. Once again, Glasson, seemingly lifeless, waits for Vashti to exit and he attacks Willie. This time he kills his rival and drags the body to the mine shaft. When Glasson returns, he immediately climbs the stairs to Vashti's room, removing his mask. Seeing his disfigured face and realizing what has happened, Vashti screams for help. Glasson strangles her.

Catherine Goulden (E.M. Lauman, 1917). A horror play with the additional theme of Mysterious Death.

A servant of a cruel master who has mysteriously disappeared, Catherine Goulden is suspected of his murder and interrogated. Although she denies the charge, under questioning Catherine admits that she had once dreamed of killing her master with a hatchet. Just then her master returns, furious that his servant dreamt of murdering him. He throws her out of the house and strikes her with a cane. It is winter and Catherine's anger and hatred are fanned into flames.

At the Break of Day (André de Lorde and Jean Bernac, 1921). *A horror play with the additional themes of Guilt, Imprisonment, and Insanity. The original ending of this play, which showed the main character being guillotined on the stage, was changed on the order of the High Commissioner of Police after much debate in the Parisian press.*

A murderer awaits his execution in a prison cell. In a fit of jealousy, he strangled his girl friend. His cellmate turns out to be the girl's father. Everyday the old man torments the condemned man with elaborate descriptions of the guillotine's preparations. Finally the half-crazed murderer is led to his beheading.

The Coffin of Flesh (André de Lorde and Henri Bauche, 1924). *A horror play with the additional themes of Cuckoldry, Hypnosis, Mysterious Death, and Surgery.*

Four English doctors have formed a club to determine whether the soul can live without the body. At one of their seances, Henderson's dead mother appears, which causes Henderson to have a stroke. Murphy, whose wife is Henderson's lover, decides to use this occasion to hypnotize the weakened Henderson into a novel physical state between life and death. The remaining doctors prepare for a surgical operation. But when one of them cuts into Henderson, no blood flows from the incision. Before they can draw any conclusions, an arm from the drapes reaches out and strangles Murphy. The corpse of Henderson then falls from the operating table with a clenched hand.

The Maker of Monsters (Max Maurey, Charles Hellem, Pol d'Estoc, 1929). *A horror play with the additional themes of Helplessness, Insanity, and Mutilation.*

A mad scientist, Dr. Brockau, has created a menagerie of freak animals, which he has given various human traits and physical resemblances. He exhibits them in a traveling circus show. His great project is to transform a gorilla, which he keeps in the corner of his tent, into a man. One night, Brockau invites Lina, a circus woman, into his tent and attempts to seduce her. The caged gorilla becomes jealous and interrupts the doctor's undertaking with grunting sounds. To punish both the gorilla and Lina—for her resistance to his love-making—Brockau announces that he will disfigure Lina's beautiful face. Although terrified, Lina manages to maneuver Brockau into the corner of the tent where the gorilla can reach out of his cage and strangle his tormentor.

"Lea strangles General Gregoroff,
the tormentor of her brother."
—*from* The Dead Rat, Room No. 6

COMEDIES AND FARCES

BOURGEOIS MORALITY

Scruples (Octave Mirbeau, 1902). *A comedy.*

Late at night, a highly sophisticated thief and his assistant have broken into the house of a connoisseur of art. The victim discovers the thieves and calls the police. While they wait for the authorities, the thief praises the tastes of the owner and explains how an intelligent man like himself becomes a house thief. He had tried many other professions, including business and politics, and found that stealing was the most honest and gentlemanly. The victim becomes so taken with the thief's style and philosophy that he waves away the chief of police when he arrives and invites the thief and his valet to breakfast. Exiting, the thief declines, saying that, in his silk hat and dress suit, he is improperly attired for the morning meal.

The Serious Little Maid (Timmory and Manoussi, 1904). *A farce with the additional theme of Prostitution.*

An old provincial couple are looking for a maid servant. They read an advertisement in a Paris newspaper of an agency that provides girls. In response to their answer, the agency man brings a very pretty little prostitute. There is a misunderstanding when the woman of the house speaks to the girl, who inquires if the service in the house is hard. The woman, who is old and haggard, tells her they have many guests in the house that she helps out with the service. The young prostitute is amazed.

An Ambitious Man (Miguel Zamacois, 1906). *A farce.*

Georges, a struggling young doctor,

begins his practice by unethically finding patients in the waiting room of an eminent doctor. All of Georges' remedies are ridiculous. A man who complains about a stomach disorder is told to remove his tie clip. Another whose rheumatism will not allow him to reach to the top of his closet is advised to lower his shelves. A wealthy widow who wishes to ask the doctor about the wisdom of remarrying becomes convinced to wed Georges. When the real doctor's valet comes into the waiting room, he asks for some medical advice from Georges, although he knows that he is a phony. Since the young doctor was about to pay the valet his agreed bribe, Georges merely deducts an amount from the valet's fee.

The Chauffeur (Max Maurey, 1908). *A classical Grand Guignol social farce about employers and modernity.*

Monsieur Nock has purchased an expensive automobile but does not know how to drive it. Nock hires Alcime, a gardener, to be his chauffeur. Alcime, who does not know how to drive either, is supposed to pick up Monsieur Filfer, a prospective buyer. Terrified, Alcime declares that the car is not operative. Nock and his wife look under the automobile and Alcime hands them tools. A crooked mechanic comes and takes away the steering wheel. Finally, Filfer arrives angry that no one has come to meet him. Filfer decides to buy the automobile only with the condition that Alcime be his personal chauffeur.

At the Cosy Corner (Frederic Boutet, 1913). *A farce.*

Twenty years ago, the owner of a cafe

outside Paris was murdered. Since then the owner's son has taken over and the cafe has prospered. Now the murderer has returned to the sight of his crime and confesses to the son. The son is distraught for two reasons: here he has discovered his father's murderer but also news of the crime will once again hurt his business. He makes a deal with the murderer.

Led by the Nose, or Nounouche (Henri Duvernois, 1919). *A farce.*

Benjamin is married to a thoroughly disagreeable wife, Bichette, who "leads him around by the nose." Rather than work for such an unpleasant mistress, their current servant quits. Bichette refuses to cook and Benjamin has to patronize cafes that he can ill afford. Benjamin's old nurse appears and is hired on as the new cook. The nurse bosses Benjamin around mercilessly, but places the house in order, and puts Bichette into her proper place.

The Recommendation (Max Maurey, 1920). *A farce.*

A poor man calls on the Director of a Paris bank to ask for a job. He brings with him the usual letter of recommendation. An underclerk takes the letter but hides it in his own pocket. The confused applicant has to explain to the banker his quest of a job. The official asks for the letter of recommendation. The job-seeker does not know how to tell the Director that his underclerk has stolen it. But because the applicant is the first person to come to the Director without such a document, the banker shows keen delight and hires him for a high position.

On the Bench (Charles Henry Hirsch, 1920). *A popular curtain-raiser farce.*

A young man from the provinces falls in love with a Parisian dressmaker. They hold a rendezvous on a bench in the Luxembourg Gardens. The youth begs the girl to spend Sunday with him in the country—and not to worry about catching the last train home. An old man sitting beside them overhears the young man's seduction plan and asks why they do not marry. The girl is willing. The young man is unwilling since the dressmaker is not of his station in life. The old man tells them of a similar situation from his own youth, which ruined both his life and his sweetheart's. Reacting to the story, the dressmaker decides not to go to the Sunday outing and lose her virtue.

Sauce for the Goose (Robert Dieudonné, 1921). *A sex farce.*

André Galoyer has been engaged for four years to Henriette. He is now preparing to confess that during this time he has already married someone else. When Henriette arrives, he is hardly able to get a word out before she confesses that she is now engaged to another man. André becomes furious and reproaches her for her outrageous behavior. André now claims that it is in order for him to marry another. For the life of him, the upset André cannot understand how Henriette would leave him for another man.

The Fox (Pierre Wolff, 1925). *A farce.*

An ex-drama critic turns thief and is caught in the act of robbing a playwright. His charm and endearing melancholy win the playwright over. The thief uses flattery to capitalize on the moment. The mediocre playwright, delighted with the critic's

compliments of his plays, offers him a meal. Then, by acting out a scene of a work-in-progress—in which a father is sweet-talked into giving his son-in-law money—the foxy thief walks off with 1,000 of the writer's francs.

I Want You to Go to Sleep (Georges Feydeau, 1940). *A farce with the additional themes of Hypnosis and Vengeance.*

The young master Boriquet is unknowingly under the spell of his evil valet Justin, who has hypnotized him into doing all the household work. Before Boriquet's fiancee, Emillienne, and her father, Doctor Valencourt, come to visit, Justin hypnotizes Boriquet into insulting them so his power over his master can continue uninterrupted. Doctor Valencourt, however, suspects something and hypnotizes Justin into confessing his perfidity. Boriquet's trance is broken and he is reunited with his Emillienne. Justin is punished by repeating endlessly that he is bad.

CUCKOLDRY

Tics (René Berton, 1908). *A sex farce.*

A man confesses to his weekend host, a doctor, that after sexual intercourse he always suffers from an embarrassing twitch. The doctor assures him that many people develop such noticeable tics after making love. Afterwards the guest accompanies the doctor's wife into her bedroom, while the doctor "examines" the man's wife in his private office. The chauffeur and maid also go off together. When they reassemble in the living room, all of them attempt to conceal their nervous tics. Not knowing what to do, the doctor blames the maid for

everything and fires her.

Madame Aurelie (Yves Mirande, 1909). *A sex farce with the additional theme of Bourgeois Morality.*

Madame Aurelie, a bearded lady in the circus, is having an affair with an effeminate young man. Her husband, leading a police escort, rushes into the room to expose her deceit. The naked Aurelie hides behind the window drapes, which draws an appreciative audience from outside the hotel. Sensing an advertising coup, Aurelie's husband drops the charges and plans to integrate the unfortunate situation into a circus sketch.

A Third Act (Serge Veber, 1921). *A farce with the additional theme of Vengeance.*

Two young authors are collaborating on a play. Robert is courting Marcel's wife Madeleine, who feels that Robert has much more talent than her husband. She plays with great spirit a love scene that Robert is reading to her and at this moment Marcel enters the room to discuss the ending of the third act. Marcel wants a strong ending; Robert and Madeleine wish a happy ending. Marcel, quick to understand, leaves them alone for a while and returns with a new scene, in which the deceived husband abandons his place to his rival. He plays the scene himself and goes out of the room leaving the lovers alone. Robert, with no desire to marry, now finds himself alone with Madeleine and realizes what is ahead of him. He is now not so sure of a happy ending after all.

Take My Lady (Max Girard, 1922). *A farce with the additional theme of Vengeance.*

A man about town has just broken up

FLATO

with his lover. He awaits his next conquest, a married woman. But, instead of the woman, her husband appears in the room. The husband drones on and on, smoking and moralizing, causing a great deal of anxiety to the lover, who is listening for the wife to enter. Finally the husband beats the lover at checkers.

SEX FARCE

Night Attack (André de Lorde and M. Masson-Forestier, 1903). *A farce in two acts with the additional theme of Cuckoldry.*

A woman comes to a provincial police station late at night. Her lover has just had a heart attack in bed. She asks the police chief to help move the body before her husband returns home from a business trip. Since she is pretty, he agrees.

At the house, they attempt to move the lifeless body but the man awakens. As soon as the policeman starts to care for the sick man, the telephone rings. It is the woman's husband calling to tell her that he will be arriving on a later train. With the approval of the woman, the officer attacks the ailing lover and drives him out of the house. The policeman takes the woman to bed.

The Seductress (Robert Dieudonné, 1914). *A farce in eight scenes.*

A woman invents stories of men pursuing her in order to incite her lover to jealous rage and action. The man's nephew is about to come to dinner. The woman tries to make her lover believe that this harmless and sexless relative is after her. To prove it to him, she convinces him to hide under the table when the nephew arrives. She practically forces the nephew to kiss her. The

lover sees through her ploy, but when she accuses the unsuspecting delivery boy of attempted seduction, the lover finally pretends to be jealous and chases the boy out of the house. At last, she is content and begs her lover not to make such a fuss.

The Short Circuit (Benjamin Rabier and Eugene Joullot, 1916). *A farce with the additional themes of Cuckoldry and Vengeance.*

A star of the music hall, Nina de Coursac, has captivated the attentions of Prince d'Inertie. The prince asks his secretary to arrange an interview with the singer at her apartment. Unfortunately, Nina's lover Robert is coming to see her the same day, so Nina must endeavor to get rid of him before the prince's interview. An electrician has been called to the apartment to repair a short circuit. There Robert bribes the electrician to impersonate the prince, while he disguises himself as the electrician. The fake prince seduces Nina so easily, that the lover and later the prince give up on her.

The Flask (Max Maurey, 1918). *A farce.*

Pierre's valet Louis gives his master, who is normally reserved and shy, a flask of a powerful aphrodisiac solution. Before Pierre can drink it, Lucette, the object of his seduction, arrives. Suddenly Pierre is called out of the room and the unsuspecting woman drinks the liquid, thinking it is a sedative. Pierre returns and frantically searches for the flask. Meanwhile Lucette has grown amorous and sexually aggressive. She cannot understand why Pierre is ignoring her for a missing bottle. Pierre then realizes what has happened and becomes horrified. Unsatisfied with his physical response to her, Lucette leaves, vowing never to return.

One Hour of Love (Charles Hellem and Pol d'Estoc, 1920). *A comedy with the additional theme of Prostitution.*

After a night out with his friends, a man takes Flora, a prostitute, back to her room, promising to pay her two weeks of rent. As an aside, upon entering her apartment, he tells the audience his plan to pay her with a counterfeit bill. He tells her that he only has one hour free before he returns home to his wife. Unfortunately, he has a habit of falling asleep right after sex. Flora promises to wake him in time, but before she can do more than loosen his clothes, the drunken man falls asleep on her bed. While he sleeps, the landlady comes in and reminds Flora of her rent due. Flora has an idea. She wakes the man up, pretends that they have already made love, and compliments him strongly on his performance. He is so happy to be told that he is a great lover that he gives her 100 real francs and runs home to his wife. Flora exclaims that being a chaste liar pays better than being an honest whore.

Alone (Henri Duvernois, 1922). *A two-act farce.*

A charming and decadent poet, Eugene, tells a friend about Mme. Hellaf-Deleponte, a woman of the world who became infatuated with him and his poetry but whom he has not seen since their meeting six months ago.

Mme. Hellaf-Deleponte finally arrives when Eugene has stepped out of his studio. She decides to hide in order to surprise him.

Eugene returns and, thinking that he is alone, acts accordingly, revealing his innately gross behavior and the fraud beneath his poetry. Then, noticing Mme. Hellaf-Deleponte behind the curtains, he launches into an emotional and sincere apology. The woman, however, has suffered no offense or disillusionment. She knows that an artist needs a great freedom of expression. As she is about to leave, Eugene then asks her to stay and go to bed with him. She takes off her hat in wordless accent.

A Not So Serious Client (Serge Veber, 1923). *A farce.*

With a heist on his mind, a thief enters a jewelry store. He is so captivated with the beautiful eyes of the salesgirl behind the counter, however, that he forgets about his plan and buys her a piece of jewelry.

To Kill Time (Max Maurey, 1923). *A farce with the additional theme of Prostitution.*

Two old ladies have opened up a "salon," or brothel, and put an ad in the newspaper to attract clients. While waiting for guests to arrive, they sit and knit and read and drink. The bell rings. One exits hurriedly to change, and the other woman greets the man at the door. He is gruff and obviously uncomfortable. The man demands to see the "women." The hostess offers him just one— her crony—who struts in dressed like a twenty-year-old, complete with wig and garish makeup. At first, he refuses her but lets himself be talked into taking her. After a brief conversation, they suddenly recognize each other: she was his nurse when he was a boy. He explains that he was merely killing time in order to appease his sick wife, who

wants him out of the house, despite his desire to care for her. He entered the "salon" only because it started to rain. The old nurse pats his hand and sends him on his way with admonishments to button up against the weather.

The Snows of D'Antan (André Mouëzy-Eon, 1926). *A two-act comedy.*

An elderly bachelor and astronomer, Rozier-Perlot, receives a telephone call from his old schoolboy chum Sauveterre. Amazingly, Sauveterre challenges the astronomer to a duel. Forty years ago, it seems they secretly shared the same mistress and Sauveterre wants to settle that score. It was so long ago, however, that neither can even remember much about her.

Rozier-Perlot and his maid, Hermine, attempt to discourage Sauveterre's foolhardy idea. To calm down the old man, Hermine tells a story about the time in life when she had two lovers. The men realize that Hermine was their mistress in school. Sauveterre calls off the duel. Hermine assures each of them privately that he was her favorite lover.

SUFFERING OF THE INNOCENT

The Cornfields (Georges Courteline, 1898). *A celebrated farce with the additional theme of Bourgeois Morality.*

An elderly bachelor in New York City, Herring desires nothing so much as absolute peace and quiet. He enters the house of the Cornfields, who at a party had invited him to spend his winter evenings. The Cornfields, however, are not the pleasant and agreeable couple he thought they were. From the first, they argue about everything,

with Herring always the innocent object of their fights. Each of the Cornfields grabs him and pulls him in the opposite direction. One after the other put so many pillows under his seat that the chair collapses. Fighting between themselves, the Cornfields inadvertently destroy his clothing, kick him in his wooden leg, throw soup in his face, shoot his artificial leg, set fire to their apartment, toss a bucket of water at him, and, as Herring exits, they invite him for a glass of champagne.

Interview (Octave Mirbeau, 1904). *A farce.*

A reporter invades a poor wine merchant's shop and submits him to a remorseless, crazed interview, inventing the most horrible and sensational stories around the man's half-uttered answers. Eventually, it is clear that the reporter takes the merchant for a wife-killer with the same last name. Refusing to believe that he could have mistaken his man, the reporter tries everything to get the merchant to confess and relate the horrid details of his crime. The reporter exits in a tirade, leaving the shop in a shambles, and the innocent merchant a nervous wreck.

The Chemist (Max Maurey, 1910). *A farce with the additional theme of Guilt.*

A woman comes to the apothecary's to buy medicine for her sick child. The chemist by mistake gives her a poisonous potion. Discovering this when the woman has gone, the chemist is frightfully upset. He turns all his customers away, including a little girl who keeps reappearing. The chemist is in terror. Again, the girl, refusing to be driven out, returns and finally succeeds in making the distracted chemist listen. It is her little brother who is the sick child. The sister returns the vial, which the chemist forgot to fill.

The Room Next Door (Robert Dieudonné, 1911). *A sex comedy.*

After a long night of cards, Jules Toussaint, a traveling salesman, is about to collapse into his hotel bed. Suddenly, he hears a knock at the door. His neighbor in the adjoining room, Dodo, begs Jules to take in his female companion, Gisele, since Dodo's wife has followed him to the hotel. Reluctantly, Jules consents, especially since Gisele has taken sole possession of his bed. When Dodo and his wife leave, Jules sends Gisele into the next room. She immediately returns, however, because she is afraid to sleep alone. Finally, Jules decides to make love to Gisele, and as soon as the light is put out Dodo comes to claim the girl. After the ruckus that quickly erupts, a man from the card game enters to pay his debt to Jules. It turns out that he is Gisele's husband. The police are brought in and Jules, the accused, is asked to leave the hotel.

The Bronze Lady and the Crystal Gentleman (Henri Duvernois, 1921). *A popular farce in two-acts with the additional themes of Helplessness, Imprisonment, Insanity and Play Transforming Into Terror.*

Monsieur Sourcier, now retired, is married to a most unpleasant wife. To gain relief from her nagging, he pretends that he is insane and has himself locked up in a private sanatorium. Now he is free to paint and be happy. Sourcier pretends that he believes that on even-numbered days he is made of delicate crystal and may break at the slightest jar; on odd-numbered days, he is tinder. Either way, absolute quiet is mandatory or he will shatter.

His wife, however, visits him twice each week. Being lonely without his company, she decides that she will pretend that she is made of bronze, a Statue of Liberty, so she can be placed in the asylum near him. Realizing that he has been outwitted, Sourcier confesses his secret to the head of the sanatorium. The doctor now is certain that both Sourciers are truly mad and has them placed under permanent confinement.

The Neglected (Max Maurey, 1928). *A comedy.*

A young man announces to his wife that he has been embezzling funds from his company and he cannot replace the money. Valiantly, she offers to sell her jewels to help replace the funds. Her diamonds, he tells her, are fakes. The concierge enters the rooms and tells them to be quiet. (It becomes apparent that they are rehearsing a play.) The couple begin to rehearse the scene again when it breaks into a real family argument. This time both the concierge and the landlord enter in a furious mood. Months shy of paying their rent, the young actors now fear that they will be thrown out of their apartment. But the landlord reassures them that he is just practicing being angry for throwing out the house guests that he is expecting next week.

"CRASS" MANNERS

Little Bugger (Oscar Méténier, 1897). *An ironic and humorous depiction of working-class life (rosse, or "crass" play) in two scenes, adapted from Méténier's short story. Also the themes of Cuckoldry, Parisian Low-life, and Vengeance.*

In the backroom of a wine shop, Eugenia tells her lover Jean, a day laborer, that he has gotten her pregnant. Jean accepts the news gleefully and attempts to cheer her up, talking of raising the "little bugger." The whining Eugenia then confesses that years ago she has married a cabinet maker, Leon Grelu. Eugenia wants to leave the shop because Grelu has reappeared in her life; she just saw him in the wine shop. Jean explodes and decides to goad Grelu into violence so Eugenia will be granted a divorce. Eugenia agrees to the plot and leaves.

Jean invites Grelu into the room for the confrontation. Instead of fighting, Grelu, a freedom-loving anarchist, toasts to Jean's proposal and leaves. Alone in the room, Jean sits confused.

Meat-Ticket (Oscar Méténier, 1897). *Another rosse play in two scenes, adapted from Méténier's short story, with the additional themes of Parisian Low-life and Prostitution.*

In the backroom of a wine shop, the Pichard family and a friend celebrate the communion of the Pichard's second daughter, Nini. The older Pichards bemoan that their first daughter, Louisa, gave them much trouble at Nini's age, running away from home. Eventually, she decided to settle down at Madame Trollon's brothel and get a "meat-ticket," a prostitute's card.

Suddenly the successful Louisa enters the room, to her family's delight. Louisa is encouraged to tell the story of her decision to become a whore: the parish priest told the Pichard children never to disobey the wishes of their parents, no matter what they are. Nini explains that she too will get her "meat-ticket" when she becomes of age. The mother Pichard concludes that even parish priests can have a good influence on the family.

Mademoiselle Fifi (Oscar Méténier, 1897). *Produced over two thousand times, this adaptation from Guy de Maupassant's short story was one of the most popular plays of the Grand Guignol. A drama with the additional themes of Bourgeois Morality and Prostitution.*

In a French provincial town during the Franco-Prussian war of 1870, German officers and French prostitutes engage in a wild party. In the midst of the celebration, a prostitute, Rachel, stabs a young German officer with a dinner knife. As the blood pours from his chest, Rachel escapes, knocking over a candelabra. In the cast of strange shadows, the Germans quietly and ritually place their dying fellow officer on the champagne-laden table. It is an ironic moment. Suddenly, the once silent bells of the town church ring. The murderer Rachel is now a heroine. France has defeated Germany.

Him (Oscar Méténier, 1897). *An example of the early genre of dramatized news items from the tabloids that featured macabre or shocking stories (faits divers). A play with the additional theme of Prostitution.*

In a cheap Parisian hotel, a prostitute, Violette, and her madame are reading a story aloud from the newspaper. A brutal killer, Martinet, is on the loose. After robbing an old woman in her apartment, he murdered her in a grisly fashion, nearly severing her head from her body with a huge knife. While the two read a list of the items that Martinet has taken from the woman, a customer arrives for Violette. The madame departs. As the the man undresses and begins to take out the contents of his bag, Violette slowly realizes that her client is the sadistic Martinet. Eventually, with the assistance of her madame, Violette gets the murderer drunk and into bed. Meanwhile the police are notified and come to arrest Martinet.

The Microbe Merchant, or the Girl With the Ovaries (Henry Céard and H. de Weindel, 1898). *This was the first of offensive Grand Guignol dramas that truly shocked newspaper critics.*

A well-meaning doctor sets himself up as a charlatan. One client comes to buy a poison to kill his father, and another man buys poison to kill his son. The charlatan sells them both harmless potions. Next a young woman arrives who has been told by a lover that she must have her ovaries removed for her to be "safe for love," and demands that he perform the operation. He refuses. The two clients return, complaining bitterly and threatening to inform the police of his quackery. The young woman realizes the doctor's good intentions, falls in love, and decides to marry him.

An Affair of Morals (Charles Esquier, 1902). *A drama with the additional themes of Prostitution and Vengeance.*

A highly-successful judge is having a private dinner party with two prostitutes. One of the women, whose lover has been sentenced by the judge, threatens to expose him. The judge suffers a fatal heart attack. The waiter brings in a doctor who has been carousing in the cafe below. The young doctor is aghast: the judge was his father. Since there is no backway, the only solution to avoid a scandal is to carry the dead judge out as if he were drunk. The waiter and doctor support him by his arms as the prostitutes hysterically sing the "Firemen's Anthem."

GUILT

The White Madness (Henri-René Lenormand, 1905). *A two-act drama with the additional theme of Helplessness.*

Marc and his fiancee are about to scale a difficult Alpine slope. They discuss what would happen if the other one fell from the mountain in the morning. Marc's fiancee says that she would cut the rope between them to save herself. Marc maintains the opposite: he would never sever the rope; he would rather die with her.

The next day they climb the mountain during a storm. On the hotel's terrace, Marc's parents nervously watch them through a telescope. Marc's fiancee slips and falls off the slope. He cuts the rope and lets her hurl through space. Then in remorse, Marc jumps off the slope into the "white madness."

Under the Red Light (Maurice Level and Etienne Rey, 1911). *A drama in three acts with the additional theme of Insanity.*

The mistress of Philippe Garnier, Therese Vaugeois, has died of influenza after only two days of sickness. A hurried medical

examiner advises that she must be buried immediately to prevent the epidemic from spreading further. Garnier blames himself for her death since he allowed Vaugeois to go to the countryside where she contracted the disease. As a final memento, Garnier takes a photograph of his mistress' face.

After the funeral Garnier's friends, Suzanne and Didier, attempt to comfort him, but Garnier is inconsolable. He must see Vaugeois' face again. Using a photographer's red light, Garnier develops the negative that he took. In the photographic image, Vaugeois' eyes are open. The magnesium flash produced a living response in her. Insanely, Garnier shouts that Vaugeois was not dead.

At the cemetery, Vaugeois' corpse is exhumed before Didier and the medical examiner. Her face is bloody from a violent struggle to rip open the coffin. Evidently, Vaugeois awoke from a coma after the burial and died only a few hours ago. When Garnier enters the graveyard, Didier sobbingly tells his friend that his mistress was truly dead.

On the Slab (André de Lorde and Georges Montignac, 1923). *A psychological drama with the additional themes of Insanity and Parisian Low-life.*

A young *apache* is arrested for killing a soldier. He is taken to the Paris morgue, where he sees the soldier's body on a slab. Still he denies having committed the crime. Knowing the young criminal is an alcoholic, the detective Poirel locks him in the room with the covered cadaver and a bottle of whiskey. Once the *apache* has polished off the bottle, he begins to hallucinate that the body has moved. Immediately, the street tough attacks the corpse with the empty bottle, screaming, "This time, I'll really kill you!" Listening from outside the room, the police come in and arrest him.

The Red Inn (Serge Basset, 1934). *A psychological drama with the additional theme of the Suffering of the Innocent.*

A young French officer has been accused of murdering a traveling German salesman. The basis of the evidence against him has been supplied by a night watchman who saw the killing through a window. Just as the soldier is being led away to a firing squad, the watchman realizes that the military emblem on the condemned man's sleeve is of a different sort. Actually, one of the officers who helped the watchman convict the soldier is the murderer. The watchman attempts to inform the head of the firing squad. He is too late. The innocent soldier has been executed.

The Visitor (André de Lorde and Henri Bauche, 1916). *A psychological drama with the additional theme of Bourgeois Morality.*

Two women, the wife of a soldier and his secret mistress, await news of his safety. There is a strained atmosphere as each plays out her assigned social role. Finally, a strange woman arrives, who reveals the man's death on a battlefield.

INJUSTICE

The Catwalk (Robert Francheville, 1913). *A drama with the additional themes of Bourgeois Morality and Imprisonment.*

A prison guard is having an affair with a female convict. Thinking that someone is about to catch them and expose their illicit relationship, he takes out his gun and fatally shoots her. When the prison authorities rush in to investigate the gunplay, the guard maintains that he fired at the prisoner to prevent her escape. Satisfied with his explanation, they promise him an immediate promotion.

The Woman Who Was Acquitted (André de Lorde, 1919). *A drama with the additional themes of Bourgeois Morality and Hypnosis.*

In his chamber after a trial, the Judge complains to his friend, the Doctor, about the jury's verdict. They have acquitted a governess who was a suspect in the strangulation murders of three children in three different families. The Judge believes that Madame Menard was guilty, but he has no proof. The Doctor urges the Judge to ask Madame Menard into his chamber. She is brought in almost against her will. Looking into her eyes and holding her wrists, the Doctor hypnotizes her. Although she will not answer any questions, Madame Menard hypnotically re-enacts the murder of the last child. Since hypnotism holds no sway in a French court and since the trial is over, Madame Menard is allowed to walk out into freedom, where the Judge predicts she will continue to strangle children.

The Sound of the Gong (Jack Jouvin, 1931). *A psychological drama with the additional themes of Bourgeois Morality and Guilt.*

The naive and innocent governess of a bourgeoise family returns to their household after spending a year in prison for neglect of duty. Answering her mistress' bell, she temporarily left the two children alone. During her absence the younger of the two children, a favored little girl, was found drowned in a reflecting pool. The governess' reappearance after the year of the drowning and trial causes Robert, the dead girl's brother, to confess that it was he, out of jealousy, who drowned his sister. The grandfather in the family, however, rejects the boy's confession and convinces him that it was all really an accident.

ON THE TELEPHONE

*by André de Lorde
and Charles Foley
(1902)*

André Marex says good-bye to his family at their isolated vacation home.

After dinner
at the Rivoire's,
Marex takes his
brandy and dessert.

Marex' wife calls to tell him that she has been hearing noises around the house. Marex assures her that they are imaginary. Later, Marex receives a second telephone call from his wife. While talking to her, Marex hears the sounds of her being brutalized and his son being murdered by tramps.

photo documentation of

A CRIME IN THE MADHOUSE

by André de Lorde
and Alfred Binet
(1925)

In the cell of an insane asylum, three lunatics surround the innocent and fearful Louise during her last night in the institution.

Hunchback, the Normandy Woman and One-Eye gag Louise, whom they believe has imprisoned a cuckoo bird behind her eyes.

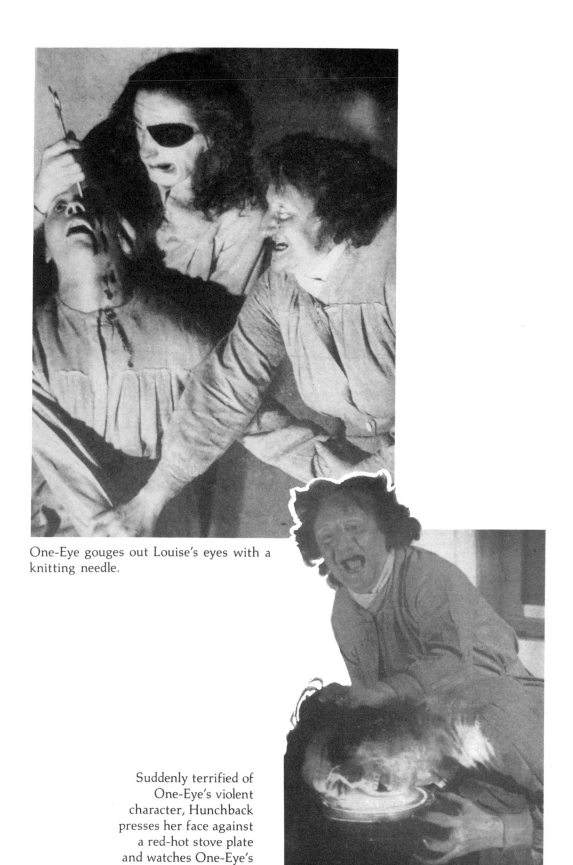

One-Eye gouges out Louise's eyes with a knitting needle.

Suddenly terrified of One-Eye's violent character, Hunchback presses her face against a red-hot stove plate and watches One-Eye's face sizzle away.

photo documentation of

ORGY IN THE LIGHTHOUSE

by Leopold Marchand
(1956)

A wild sailor, Yves, brings two prostitutes, Rosa and Nini, into his brother's lighthouse on the Breton coast.

Logonadee, the old, drunken keeper of the lighthouse, watches as Nini prepares to dance with Yves.

Later that night, Yves and Nini make love.

During their orgy,
the beacon of the lighthouse
goes out and a boat flounders
among the rocks below.
Blaming their predicament on
Rosa's theft of a religious icon,
Yves cuts her throat.

It is discovered that the
destroyed boat carried
the boy's mother. In a
frenzy of repentance,
Yves and his brother
burn Nini to death.

FEAR IN LITERATURE

by André de Lorde

EITHER ACTOR NOR DIRECTOR, ANDRÉ de Lorde was the dominant figure in the Grand Guignol's history. Dubbed the "Prince of Terror," de Lorde wrote many of its most popular plays which he quickly anthologized together with important statements and analyses on the genre of theatrical horror. An intellectual and amateur scientist, de Lorde articulated and coyly justified the Grand Guignol's exploration into such taboo and artistically lowbrow subjects as insanity, incest, race hatred, murder, and bodily mutilation. Beginning with Dr. Goudron and Professor Plume *in 1903, de Lorde's dramas were staples of the Grand Guignol's predilection for unexpected violence and sexual hysteria. In de Lorde's seemingly naturalistic world, madness was a human constant that had the power to overthrow any social contract at any time, be it bourgeois authority or familial bonding. De Lorde's plays achieved an enormous following in Paris and beyond because they reminded their audiences and readers that torturous thoughts and brute violence are always lurking behind the most innocent of relationships. Nothing in life is really certain.*

An entire literature of Fear exists.

Why should this be astonishing? Each one of us has in his innermost being a secret longing for violent emotions. At all times, in all parts of the globe, horror shows have drawn large audiences. The huge amphitheaters in Rome were too small to hold the citizens eager to see the gladiators slaughter one another and the Christians thrown to the lions. If the Inquisition had made public its interrogations conducted on the rack, they would have had to turn people away. To witness the hideous torture of Damiens, the crowd surged toward the square as though to holiday festivities.

"Bah!" you will say, "Times have changed; in our days, the progress of civilization has made such barbarous pastimes unthinkable." True enough. Still, set men, bulls, and horses at one another in an arena, and excited spectators will shriek with joy; at break of day guillotine some human wreck half-dead with fright, and there won't be enough soldiers, their bayonets fixed, to hold back the pushing throng of those who want to see. And don't those tender hearts, who are revolted by such spectacles, seek out at fairs the most violent and horrific "attractions"? Don't they derive acute pleasure at the circus or music hall from watching the most dangerous feats? If I perspire with anxiety as I follow the movements of the dancer along the tightrope, if my breathing stops with the music when this young person in pink tights is about to attempt what she herself calls the death leap, it is because I actually imagine an atrocious death for her, her battered corpse bloodying the sand in the ring. No doubt, if I were sure that the accident was going to happen, I would be the first to rush forward to prevent it; but if, on the other hand, I was certain that it would not happen, I would lose interest in the show. A most curious compromise on the part of our consciences is at work here. If my sensibility steps forth to reproach me for the odious satisfaction that I find in thus anticipating a calamity, I immediately assuage these scruples by involving the law of probabilities. There is only one chance in a thousand that the accident will happen precisely today; but as soon as this reassuring thought runs the risk of dulling my pleasure, I revive it again by calling up in my mind's eye the image of the fall, despite what seems possible. I would not be as ferocious as that Englishman who went to every show of a wild animal act in order to be present when the lion tamer would get eaten; but, by going once quite by chance, I have the slight hope, without admitting it to myself, that today will be the day, more or less in the same way that I dream—without daring to believe it—that my lottery ticket will be the winning one. . . .

Fear has always existed, and each century has stamped upon its literature the mark of the fears that tormented it, but the primitive caveman and the contemporary businessman have not shuddered for the same reasons. The sources of fear have varied, but not fear itself, which is eternal and immutable. . . .

Feeble as they are, the Gothic novels had a real vogue; not only were Anne Radcliffe and Monk Lewis imitated by a host of minor writers, they also had the honor of inspiring two of England's greatest writers, Walter Scott and Lord Byron, to write many a picturesque descriptive passage. In France, *The Monk* and *The Mysteries of Udolpho*, translated in 1797, were read, appreciated, and plagiarized; the novelists, from Ducray-Duminil to Eugene Sue, went to them for stirring subjects for many, many years, and the playwrights along the Boulevard of

André de Lorde

Crime brought to the stage the principal episodes of these works.

As early as 1799, Guilbert de Pixérécourt, the father of melodrama, staged at the Ambigu his *Chateau des Appennins*, borrowed from Anne Radcliffe's novel, but where the horror is considerably attenuated. This astute dramatist knew how to turn a famous novel to good profit in the theater; he neglected no "effect" capable of moving or astounding the spectators: *Victor, Ou l'Enfant de la Foret, L'Homme a Trois Visages, Le Monastere Abandonne*, quite like *Le Chateau des Appennins*, are full of ingenious situations. In one of his plays, *Christophe Colomb, ou la decouverte de Nouveau Monde* (1814), whose action in part unfolds in the Antilles, Pixérécourt, on the look-out for novelties, was even convinced that he should, "for the sake of greater verisimilitude," have his savages speak the language of the Antilles taken from Father Breton's Caribbean dictionary. The results are not without savor, as witness this piece of dialogue between King Oranko and his subject Kavaka:

ORANKO: Cati louma.
KAVAKA: Amouliaca asackia Kereber
           (Oranko hesitates).
ORANKA: Inolaki...Chicalama. . . .
KAVAKA: Hava a moutou Koule
           Ouekelli.
ORANKA: Areskoui, azakia, kavaiti
           avou.
    ALL: Anakilika!
KAVAKA: Ouallou hougousou!

And so it goes on and on . . .for whole scenes the actors carry on the dialogue in Caribbean. . . .

The true genius of fear is, in actual fact, incarnated in Edgar Poe, and his work brings together all the seeds of terror that can blossom in the human soul: physical horrors, moral anxieties, painful apprehensions of the other world, and even this sensation previously unrecorded in literature, *the fear of being afraid*, that tortures the unfortunate Roderick Usher. The dominant trait of this exceptional talent is the conjunction of unbridled imagination and imperturbable logic, the fusion of nightmare and truth. In the midst of his most hallucinatory dreams, Poe always keeps one foot firmly planted in reality. In his work, macabre fantasy and meticulous precision conducive to verisimilitude become intertwined, overlap, and grow inseparable. There results from this union an impression of dread that no one else, not even Dante, has ever produced. As the reader enters into contact with Poe, a secret terror softly steals and glides into his soul, then takes possession of him, clasps him tightly, makes him shudder. The strongest nerves can offer no resistance; willy-nilly, we follow Poe into Hell, to which his art has been able to lend a semblance of life. First he rocks us on the waves of a raging sea, and then he suspends us on the edge of a bottomless abyss; vertigo seizes us, anguish makes our throat contract. "Panic-stricken" genius is the phrase that Barbey d'Aurevilly has used in speaking of Poe: no epithet could be more fitting. . . .

Poe's literary influence has been immense. Strangely enough, it was felt in France before showing any signs in his native country. In the second half of the nineteenth century, while Charles Nodier, Gerard de Nerval, Theophile Gautier, and Erckmann-Chatrian continue the Hoffman tradition and write fantastic rather than terrifying

works, we see the example of the American master inspire numerous disciples. . . .

His influence can be seen on many writers, including some of the greatest: above all on Baudelaire, who translated almost all of Poe and who is indelibly marked by his work; there are many poems in his *Les Fleurs Du Mal* where we catch reminiscences of Edgar Poe, and it can be asserted that without him, Baudelaire would not have realized all his capabilities.

Poe's mark is no less visible on Barbey d'Aurevilly and Villiers de l'Isle-Adam. Both read Poe (Barbey even devoted some magnificent pages to him), both have been subject to his authority; but *Les Diaboliques* and *Contes Cruels* are very far removed from Poe's *Tales of the Grotesque and Arabesque*. That is because Barbey and especially Villiers are unrepentant romantics. They can only conceive fear with a stately train of situations and antithesis in the style of Victor Hugo; the veiled figures, the funeral processions, the cloistered leper in Villiers' *Duke of Portland* are scarcely more believable than the coffins in Hugo's *Lucrece Borgia* or the drowned bodies in Dumas père's *Tour de Nesle*. All of this literary satanism is hardly frightening; it has the musty smell of old bric-a-brac and the property room.

Much more realistic in their sober precision, Merimée's novellas achieve effects of terror that strike you with unexpected rapidity like a gypsy girl's dagger. *Colombia*, *Lokis*, and *La Venus d'Ille* surpass by far in emotional intensity the best of the *Contes Cruels*. The true spiritual heir of Edgar Poe is incontestably Marcel Schwob—with the difference that separates talent from genius. Strange affinities exist between these two spirits: the same sarcastic

A typical Grand Guignol audience captured with a flash

and terrifying imagination is characteristic of each of them; they both possess the same "meditative facility" which Poe bestows upon Egaeus in the tale "Bernice." The painful anxiety of the one, and the Jewish sensibility of the other, reach by different routes the same goal. There is in Schwob's *Sur les Dentes* a ferocious irony that closely resembles Poe's "Loss of Breath" or "The Man Who Was Used Up," and *L'Homme Voile* equals in phlegmatic horror "The Cask of Amontillado". . . .

nera, circa 1954.

Writers could not simply go on imitating Poe indefinitely, still less could they outdo him. They were obliged to renew the genre. This is what has been attempted by the creators of the scientific-marvelous, a rich source of terror and delight. The progress of the sciences, the quasi-fabulous discoveries of the past thirty years, and the publicity given to research accomplished by inventors have contributed to arousing our minds to new objects of curiosity. Science has gone from the laboratory to the novel.

Jules Verne confined himself to considering as accomplished certain discoveries that already exist to all intents and purposes. Wells, Rosny the elder, and Maurice Renard go much further still: they are not concerned with what will be, but with what could be, and, boldly wielding the hypothesis, they venture out into vast expanses of the unknown. Here, it should be observed, there is no question of the supernatural, which for science does not exist. At most, they propose for our scrutiny facts susceptible to a dual interpretation, the one miraculous, the other rational (Wells' *Pollock and the Porroh Man* and Maurice Renard's *Le Singe*); the true domain of these storytellers remains the uncertain and the not-yet-known. That is how Wells imagines perilous journeys through time; that is how Rosny supposes the intrusion onto our planet of one of those invisible worlds that fill the emptiness of infinite space; that is how Maurice Renard makes us perceive the diabolical experiments conducted by Dr. Alexis Carrel. Pure imagination? No, certainly not, since such tales offer us, as applied to the study of imaginary phenomena or of monsters, the most rigorous methods of investigation. We find in Wells the study pursued with perfect logic—except in one point—of what would happen if a man succeeded in making himself invisible by the discoloration of his blood. Thus these authors create new subjects of terror, which are addressed less to the nerves than to the understanding, and which answer our desire for truth while at the same time giving sustenance to the need for shudders which is a part of our nature.

—*Translated by Daniel Gerould from* La Revue Mondiale *(March 15, 1927)*

A Drama In One Act
By André de Lorde
(1903)

Adapted from the story, "The System of
Dr. Tarr and Prof. Fether",
by Edgar Allan Poe
(1845)

(Translated from the French by Jeff Casper)

CHARACTERS:

Doctor Goudron, 45
Professor Plume, 60
Henri, 30
Jean, 28
Robert, 25
Chief Guard, 40
First Guard
Second Guard
Third Guard
Madame Joyeuse, 45
Mademoiselle Eugenie, 18

THE SYSTEM OF DOCTOR GOUDRON AND PROFESSOR PLUME

(An austerely decorated psychiatrist's study. Large French windows at back open onto a balcony. A door stage left; when opened, a long hallway is seen. A low door stage right with a fireplace near it. On the mantelpiece are several electrical devices, books, a carafe of water, etc. There is also a very messy desk, a library in one corner of the room, chairs, arm chairs, etc. A summer afternoon; bright sunlight.)

SCENE I—Henri, Jean

(Long silence as the curtain rises. Then knocking is heard at the door stage right. More silence. The knock is repeated. Then the door opens slowly. A man's head appears; he looks about the room, enters, then turns to speak to someone following him.)

HENRI: Nobody's here.

JEAN: *(entering as he speaks)* There's nobody anywhere! *(He closes the door automatically behind him.)*

HENRI: You can walk in here like it's a public park!

JEAN: Well, this sure is a strange institution! All the doors are open . . .the lunatics must be able to escape whenever they wish!

HENRI: Let's wait here . . . Someone will come soon . . . *(Looks around the room.)* This must be the director's office.

(Silence. They examine the room, the library, the electrical apparatus.)

JEAN: *(suddenly cheery)* Say, old pal—are we in the wrong place? . . . Are you sure this is it? Imagine if we've come into another place by mistake! . . . That would be funny!

HENRI: Yes, that would be funny . . .

(They both laugh. Suddenly, they are interrupted by shrill, terrifying screams from outside.)

JEAN: *(with a start)* What is that?

HENRI: *(listening, and moving to the window)* It's the patients.

JEAN: The patients . . . Do you think so?

HENRI: Who did you think it would be?

            (The screams increase to a horrifying din.)

JEAN: Those screams! What is going on?

HENRI: *(opening the window)* What do you think is going on?

JEAN: *(following him)* Do you see anything?

HENRI: *(moving out to the balcony and leaning over)* You can't see anything from this balcony . . . a large courtyard down below . . . *(leaning farther out)* Oh! We're so high up! . . . *(closing the window)* It must be the inmates making that racket, I'm certain. They often yell like that, especially in stormy weather, and there's a bad storm coming up—it's in the air. *(He wipes his brow.)*

JEAN: *(wiping his brow, too, and sitting on a corner of the desk)* You said it!

HENRI: You should hear them when it thunders! It's terrifying! You've never been to an insane asylum before?

JEAN: *(with irony)* This is the first time I've had the pleasure.

HENRI: It's very interesting!

JEAN: Yes . . . perhaps. I wouldn't be here otherwise. But really, you wanted to come, and I simply followed you.

HENRI: You won't regret it.

            (More screams are heard, as piercing as the howling of wild animals.)

JEAN: *(stands up, frightened)* Again! What are they doing to those poor people? I'm sure the guards are mistreating them horribly. It's shameful!

HENRI: Of course not! I told you, it's the storm coming on that upsets them . . . You'll see that in this institution, which is unique in

France, the patients live in nearly complete freedom and are well cared for, in a very gentle, humane manner . . .

JEAN: I've never heard of a place like that.

HENRI: It's like that here. You'll see . . .

JEAN: *(grimacing)* I'd rather not see!

HENRI: Don't be ridiculous!

JEAN: What do you want? Crazy people scare me! . . . And then those screams!

HENRI: *(teasing)* Coward!

JEAN: I'm not afraid . . . but I don't think it's going to be a very pleasant sight. Those poor devils, people come to gape at them as if they were bizarre animals! We don't have the right! They are sick just like any other patients . . . more to be pitied than the others.

HENRI: But my dear fellow, what harm do we do them by coming to see them, by giving them attention? On the contrary, it is only since we have begun to give them this attention that their plight has improved a bit, that we now treat them like other patients . . . Besides, I didn't come here for them, but for the doctor who directs the asylum. He is, it seems, a remarkable psychiatrist, know world-wide for his books and his experiments. He has a method, a system for treating the insane which has brought about marvelous cures. It's very difficult to get in here, you know.

JEAN: Oh! Tell me about it! The entrance was wide open. We climbed the stairs, and walked through the entire institution without seeing so much as a cat . . .

HENRI: *(interrupting him)* I mean, the director—a very singular fellow—very rarely authorizes visitors. Fortunately, I have a letter of recommendation for him. *(he searches his pockets)* If I haven't lost it! . . . *(finds it)* No, here it is! With this, I hope that we'll be well received . . . that we'll be shown everything. I have to get at least two articles out of this for the newspaper.

JEAN: *(smiling)* Or three. Ah, clever! *(stopping short)* Shh! Listen! . . . Someone's coming!

HENRI: None too soon!

 (They take off their hats, and take on a correct pose. Long silence. They look at each other, astonished.)

JEAN: No . . . but I thought I heard a noise, there, in the room next door . . . *(listens hard)* Yes, there is someone . . .

HENRI: *(coming closer)* You think so?

JEAN: *(pushing him toward the door stage right)* I'm positive.

 (Henri crosses the room, moves to the door and knocks.)

VOICE: *(behind the door)* Eh? Who's there?

HENRI: *(loudly)* Excuse me! Whom should one address in order to . . .

 (The door opens. Goudron enters abruptly and closes the door behind him violently. He stays there, pressed against the door. He wears the rosette medal of an officer of the Legion of Honor. His speech and movements are sharp and abrupt.)

SCENE II—Henri, Jean, Goudron

GOUDRON: Who are you? . . . What do you want?

HENRI: *(he and Jean back away from this apparition)* Excuse me, monsieur, we walked through the institution without meeting a living soul who could inform us . . .

JEAN: *(continuing)* . . .We would like to speak with the director . . .

GOUDRON: *(brutally)* The director? What do you want with him?

HENRI: We would like to visit the institution . . . We were recommended by Dr. Richard . . . Here's a note from him. *(He hands Goudron the letter.)*

GOUDRON: Ah! Ah! Very good, very good! *(He takes the letter, skims it, crumples it up, and throws it on the desk.)* I see what it's about . . . *(smiling)* You would like to receive authorization to visit the institution, to see the insane . . .

JEAN: We would be very grateful . . .

HENRI: Is it possible to see the director?

GOUDRON: *(solemnly)* The director? But I am he, gentlemen. Who did you think I was?

HENRI: I beg your pardon! I did not know that I had the honor of speaking . . .

GOUDRON: *(becoming very friendly)* Would you please sit down, gentlemen. *(He indicates two chairs.)*

HENRI: Perhaps we are disturbing you?

GOUDRON: Not in the least, gentlemen, not in the least. I am delighted to place myself entirely at your disposition.

HENRI: Thank you, monsieur.

JEAN: You're too kind, truly.

(Jean and Henri sit. Goudron, with a very conceited air, sits in the arm chair behind the desk, adopts a suitable pose, then leans back quickly.)

GOUDRON: I'm listening, gentlemen.

HENRI: This, monsieur, is what we hope to gain from your great kindness. We realize how seldom one is privileged to be allowed a detailed visit of the institution that you have directed with such authority for so many years . . .

GOUDRON: *(repeating)* For so many years! . . .

HENRI: I am a writer for the *Paris Journal*, as is my friend, Monsieur Jean Valmont. If you will permit me, I would like to take some notes

	on your institution, on the patients you attend to here, and if possible, if you would not mind too terribly, I would like to ask for information about yourself, your work, and your method of treatment, your famous system . . .
GOUDRON:	*(repeating)* My system!
JEAN:	We would be very grateful if you would grant us this favor . . .
HENRI:	*(taking a notebook and pencil from his pocket, as does Jean)* And so would our readers . . .
GOUDRON:	*(with great bombast)* Gentlemen, I am very flattered, . . . very flattered, that you have had the idea of visiting me and that you are interested in a work that is dear to me and that has been my life since I was brought here . . . The system of which you have heard—and which has cost me much pain and anguish—is, in effect, my invention. I believe it is destined to have a powerful effect on the minds of the insane. *(With increasing grandiloquence)* Ah! Gentlemen! The insane! Who will tell of their suffering, their misery! Until now, they have been treated like vermin, like strange beasts, and not like patients. *(More and more emphatic)* Pity them! Care for them, gentlemen! Humanity demands it, science commands it!
HENRI:	*(aside to Jean)* Charlatan!
GOUDRON:	I do not think that I offend the modesty of a simple scholar secluded from the world by telling you that I have, up until now, obtained very interesting cures, indeed, of which I am presently collecting the observations in order to submit them to the Faculty of Medicine . . . *(insistently)* Yes, gentlemen, to the Faculty of Medicine. I could even cite for you . . . *(At this moment, what sounds like groaning is heard: it seems to be coming from the room stage left. Goudron stops, looks toward the door stage left, listens.)* Ah! I still hear him! *(The groaning grows more distinct. Goudron rises.)* Excuse me, gentlemen . . . *(He goes to the door stage left and abruptly takes a stand before it. In a loud voice:)* Now, you shut up, my friend! When will you stop moaning? *(as if he were suddenly responding to someone)* What good do you think it will do? I'm the master, do you hear? Not you! I want you to be quiet! *(He pounds on the door with his fist, then turns, smiling,*

to Jean and Henri, who have watched the scene with astonishment.) One really must speak to him like that . . . Pardon me, I beg of you . . . It's a poor lunatic that I cannot seem to calm.

JEAN: *(frightened)* Right there—next door—a lunatic?

GOUDRON: Yes, I put him there so that I could watch him. Oh! I can't leave him for a minute. I am the only one who has any influence over him . . . He's the worst case, the most dangerous . . . Yes gentlemen, the most dangerous! *(pause)* But what were we saying?

HENRI: We were speaking of the absolutely remarkable results of your system . . .

                 (Goudron paces nervously about the room while Henri takes notes and Jean, unnerved, glances over from time to time at the door stage left.)

GOUDRON: Yes! My system! Well, gentlemen, you must already be familiar with my system in a general way, if not in its detail. You have, without a doubt, heard about the essential and the most interesting part of the treatment that I apply to the patients here—treatment, by the way, that is already being applied in all of Germany, England, and Italy, and that, I would hope, will soon be used world-wide. My system—as it is vulgarly called on the outside, as if, gentlemen, it were actually a practical invention—my system . . .

                 (More groans are heard from the room stage left. Goudron stops abruptly, and looks toward the room.)

GOUDRON: He's at it again! . . . What a beast! *(furious)* However, this noise must cease!

                 (He crosses to the door quickly, and disappears into the room stage left, violently slamming the door behind him.)

SCENE III—Jean, Henri alone

                 (A pause. The reporters look at each other.)

HENRI: What a strange man.

JEAN: Bizarre face, intelligent . . .

HENRI: Yes, but what a quack! "My system!" He's full of himself!

JEAN: He's delighted that we've come to interview him. You were very clever!

             (A horrible scream is heard, followed by harsh laughter. The reporters jump up, terrified. Then Goudron reappears, very calm.)

JEAN: *(approaching Goudron)* What is it?

HENRI: What's going on?

SCENE IV—Jean, Henri, Goudron

GOUDRON: Nothing, gentlemen, nothing . . . *(smiling)* He won't bother us again . . . I've calmed him down. What a brute! Here, look how he scratched me! . . . Go on, look! He's a vicious one, the devil! *(shows his hands.)*

JEAN: Oh! He's destroyed your hands!

HENRI: They're scratched to pieces!

GOUDRON: *(wiping his hands with his handkerchief)* Oh, it's nothing. I've seen much worse since I've been here!

JEAN: With patients like that, you must often be in real danger . . .

GOUDRON: Yes, we have a hard time of it! He's very intelligent when he's not having one of his fits; but this patient has a mania that nothing up till now has been able to cure, despite the years he has spent being cared for here . . . *(smiling)* With all his might he wants to become a doctor and run this institution . . . *(offering them cigarettes from a box on the desk.)* He has a ferocious hatred for me! Not more than half an hour ago, he succeeded in inciting the rest of the inmates to revolt! These others, who fear him terribly and obey him like a chief, fell upon us quite unexpectedly. They wanted to imprison us in their own cells. We had a difficult time getting out of that jam, and bringing them back to reason. *(laughing)* If one can really say, gentlemen, that one can bring a madman back to reason . . . It was a terrible battle between them and us!

HENRI: *(to Jean)* Those were the screams we heard!

GOUDRON: *(continuing in a cheery tone)* In any case, now they are locked up, and locked up well. As for the "Director," as everyone here calls him, I had placed him there *(indicating the room off left)* in order to keep him calm. But he made such a noise! And I can't stand noise . . . *(repeating in a strange voice)* Yes, gentlemen, I can't stand noise . . . *(pause. He sits.)* It was necessary to punish him very severely, despite the repugnance that I have always felt for treating the patients in that manner. *(moved)* It hurt me deeply!

HENRI: Did you put him in a straitjacket?

GOUDRON: Ah! Don't talk about that! Really, why do you mention that?

HENRI: *(abashed)* But I thought . . .

GOUDRON: *(furious)* Straitjacket! But that's horrible! It's monstrous! . . . You'll drive me crazy!

HENRI: *(trying to mend his error)* I know that you are hardly a partisan to these severe methods of repression . . .

GOUDRON: Barbarous! Vile!

JEAN: Yet, nevertheless, in certain cases . . .

HENRI: It is necessary to use it as a last resort . . .

JEAN: Or the showers . . .

GOUDRON: *(slamming the table)* Really, gentlemen, what are you saying! The showers! But that's even worse than the straitjacket! That cold water beating violently against your head and body . . . *(shuddering)* Brr! It's like throwing oil on a fire! It's obvious you don't know what it's like! Oh! Let's talk no more of that, I beg of you.

(He takes his head in his hands, as if he were suffering. A long embarrassed

silence. Jean and Henri look at one another, stupefied. They seem to be asking each other: "What is the matter with him?")

HENRI: *(after a pause)* Could you, sir, go into some details of the new method you use?

GOUDRON: *(suddenly becoming very friendly and calm again)* Of course, gentlemen, of course . . . Isn't that why you've come . . . *(The door stage right opens and there appears a small timid old man, followed shortly by a young man and two ladies. They enter slowly, one at a time, without a word, smiling.)* . . . But here is Monsieur Plume . . . and Monsieur Robert. I will be happy to present them to you. They are highly valued collaborators of mine, and precious friends. *(To the reporters, who have risen.)* Don't disturb yourselves, please, don't bother.

SCENE V—Jean, Henri, Goudron, Robert, Plume, Mme. Joyeuse, Mlle. Eugenie

([The following is de Lorde's footnote, probably describing the characters as played by the original cast:] Each of these new characters should have a tic or a mad habit that is not too obvious. Mme. Joyeuse holds a flower which she frequently brings to her nose; Mlle. Eugenie's eyes have a nervous tic—she blinks often; Plume looks off into space, with a beatific grin; and Robert, three or four times during the scene, searches his pockets rapidly as if he has lost something, then reverts to the immobility of a statue.)

GOUDRON: *(moving eagerly to the newcomers)* Good day, gentlemen. Ladies, you may enter. Don't be scared. These gentlemen are reporters who have heard of our institution and who wish to visit it.

MME. JOYEUSE: *(a coquette, rose in hand, making a deep curtsy)* Really, gentlemen, have you come to see the insane? Does that interest you?

(The reporters smile and bow.)

GOUDRON: Permit me, gentlemen, to introduce to you the celebrated Professor Plume, my excellent friend and very distinguished colleague.

PLUME: *(bowing in a grotesque manner)* My dear director! . . . Gentlemen . . .

GOUDRON: *(continuing the presentations)* My friend, M. Robert, and these ladies . . . But I beg of you, do sit down. We'll show the unfortunate patients to these gentlemen in a little while, after they have calmed down a bit.

PLUME: *(repeating)* Calmed down! . . .

(Everyone sits.)

MME. JOYEUSE: Oh! I do hope these gentlemen will have a pleasant time! I never could look a madman in the face, myself.

JEAN: *(to Henri, softly)* What's she doing here?

MLLE. EUGENIE: *(To Mme. Joyeuse)* What an amusing sort of entertainment!

HENRI: *(in a low voice, to Jean, indicating Goudron)* His wife and daughter, no doubt!

MLLE. EUGENIE: Insanity! What a horrible illness!

PLUME: *(repeating)* Horrible! . . .

MME. JOYEUSE: Oh! Gentlemen, you scientists must quickly find a cure for this terrible scourge of humanity!

GOUDRON: *(solemnly)* We're searching.

PLUME: *(repeating)* We're searching.

JEAN: *(to Henri, watching Plume)* He's funny, that old professor!

HENRI: *(to Goudron, flattering him)* But sir, thanks to your system . . .

JEAN: *(embellishing)* . . . your admirable system . . .

HENRI: Marvelous system!

GOUDRON: *(modestly)* Ah, gentlemen, I do not merit such praise . . . In any case, I don't merit it all alone. Associate, if you please, my very dear and eminent colleague, the Professor Plume . . .

PLUME: *(bowing again grotesquely)* My dear director . . .

GOUDRON: The method I have employed for treating the patients—a method that I have called the "system of soothing"—is my invention. But this method was very considerably modified in certain parts by my renowned friend . . . *(he motions to Plume)* The treatment to which we submit our patients, gentlemen, is perfectly simple: we do not contradict any of their whims. On the contrary: not only do we indulge them, we even encourage them. This is how we have brought about a certain number of radical cures . . . Approximately sixty percent.

JEAN: *(writing)* Sixty percent?

HENRI: *(also writing)* Really, in that proportion?

GOUDRON: Absolutely! There is no reasoning that affects the feeble reason of a madman more than the "reductio ad absurdum." We have had, for example, patients who believed they were chickens. Their treatment consisted of the following: to recognize, and to accept their mania as a positive fact, and from that time on to give the patient, during an entire week, the food that is properly fed to a chicken. Thanks to this system, a few kernels of corn and a bit of gravel are enough to work miracles . . . *(he laughs)* Corn . . . a bit of gravel! Ha! Ha!

             (They all laugh.)

JEAN: *(also laughing)* Very curious!

HENRI: *(laughing)* That's extremely funny!

GOUDRON: But this incomparably humane system, nevertheless, presents a danger, a great danger! It is not possible to guess, to anticipate the caprice of a lunatic. It is never very prudent to let them walk about freely, without any surveillance . . . The madman, gentlemen, can be *soothed*, as they say, for a time; but he is always, in the end, capable of wildness. What's more, his guile is proverbial. He really is very tricky! If he has a plan in mind, he knows how to hide it with marvelous hypocrisy.

PLUME: *(repeating)* Marvelous.

(During this scene, from Plume's line on, we should feel the rumble of the storm in the distance increase up until thunder claps; the actors should show the heat that weighs in the air and begins to unnerve them.)

HENRI: At this time, sir, do you have many patients?

GOUDRON: Half a dozen, in all.

JEAN: Not more?

GOUDRON: They count for three times that number, you can believe it! They've given us more trouble, just those six . . .

HENRI: Out of those six, there are more women than men, I suppose?

GOUDRON: They are all men. And strapping, hearty fellows, I can assure you! Ha, ha!

(He breaks into a noisy laugh. Plume, Robert, Joyeuse, and Eugenie join in, even more noisily.)

JEAN: *(low, to Henri)* What makes them laugh like that?

HENRI: *(to Goudron)* I had always heard it said that there were more lunatics among women than among men.

MME. JOYEUSE: *(simpering)* Oh, sir! What are you saying? That is an affirmation that is as false as it is unfriendly to our sex.

HENRI: *(smiling)* Evidently, Madame, please excuse me! . . . But it is not a personal opinion; it is what the statistics say, and we know that they have no sense of gallantry.

MME. JOYEUSE: The statistics are wrong! More insane among women than among men! To assert such a thing is absurd! Isn't it, my dear M. Plume?

PLUME: *(repeating)* Absurd.

MME. JOYEUSE: Women, almost universally I admit, are singular, eccentric, and crotchety! But that is a long way from losing their sanity! Isn't that right, my dear director?

GOUDRON: I totally agree with you, Mme. Joyeuse.

(Hearing the bizarre name of "Mme. Joyeuse," the reporters smile to each other.)

MME. JOYEUSE: And you, Mlle. Eugenie, are you also of my opinion?

MLLE. EUGENIE: Absolutely, Mme. Joyeuse! One would have to be an ass to maintain the contrary!

GOUDRON: *(excited, laughing)* Speaking of an ass, can you imagine that we have a patient here who has taken it into his head that he is an ass!

(Robert, who has not yet said a word nor made a gesture, stands up suddenly and leaps in front of the reporters.)

ROBERT: And he's such a tiring patient! We have a hard time keeping him still. For a long time he would eat nothing but thistles. He was always busy kicking out his heels, like this . . . Watch gentlemen, like this! . . .

(He starts kicking out his heels and laughing in great bursts. While doing this, he kicks Mme. Joyeuse.)

MME. JOYEUSE: *(furious, standing up)* Monsieur Robert, I would be very much obliged if you would please contain yourself. Your jokes are in doubtful taste . . . You have ruined my brocade! These gentlemen would have understood without this demonstration.

(She sits back down, turns her back to the group.)

ROBERT: *(sitting down, ashamed)* A thousand pardons, Mme. Joyeuse . . . I had no intention of offending you . . . none at all!

GOUDRON: *(interrupting)* My dear M. Robert, the man of whom you speak was very seriously ill, but one cannot compare him to the one we all knew, with the exception of these gentlemen, of course! I'm talking about the one who thought he was a bottle of champagne, and who, when he spoke, always made a "pop, pop" and a "fizz, fizz" . . . *(he imitates a bottle of champagne being uncorked and gives an enormous bang on the table, which makes the reporters jump.)*

Just like a cork popping . . . Ha! Ha!

(He laughs inexhaustibly. The others imitate him.)

JEAN: *(in a low voice to Henri)* That laughter gets on my nerves!

HENRI: *(also low)* What's the matter with them?

ROBERT: *(still doubled with laughter)* And Bouvier?

PLUME: *(roaring with laughter)* Ah! Yes! Bouvier!

GOUDRON: *(laughing harder)* Bouvier the Top! We nicknamed him "the Top" because he had taken a fancy to believing that he had changed into a top . . .

ROBERT: You would have died laughing, gentlemen, to see him spin like a little top! . . . He would pirouette for hours on one foot. *(He crouches, and spins around quickly, imitating the Top, bursting out laughing, then he springs up suddenly.)* We had Jules Deshoulieres, too, who was really a strange case. Imagine, gentlemen, that he thought he was a pumpkin! And he was constantly hounding the cook to have himself put in hot water! . . . In hot water, gentlemen! Ha! Ha!

(He falls back in his chair, doubled with laughter, as are the others.)

JEAN: *(low, to Henri)* It's not natural.

HENRI: *(low, to Jean)* No, it is not natural.

(Mlle. Eugenie gets up abruptly and goes toward the reporters with a strange air. The two men back their chairs away, frightened.)

MLLE. EUGENIE: M. Merlin, at least, had a more sensible caprice; his mania was inspired by common sense, and it at least brought pleasure to all those who knew him . . . he discovered, upon reflection, that he had been changed, by accident, into a rooster. But as a rooster, he conducted himself quite reasonably. He flapped his wings like this! *(she imitates a rooster flapping his wings)* And as for his song, it was delicious! *(she crows like a rooster)* Cock-a-doodle-doo! Cock-a-doodle-doo!

ALL: *(except Goudron and the reporters)* Cock-a-doodle-doo! Cock-a-doodle-doo!

HENRI: *(stands up, in a low voice to Jean)* They're crazy!

JEAN: *(stands, as well. Low, to Henri)* What does this mean?

GOUDRON: *(rises, angry, bangs on the table)* Mlle. Eugenie, will you please contain yourself. If you cannot behave in a decent manner, as a young woman should, you may leave . . .

ALL: *(except Eugenie, who lowers her head and stands still in the middle of the room)* The director is right! . . . The director is right! . . . The director is right! . . .

JEAN: *(low, to Henri)* Come on, let's go. I'm sick of this!

HENRI: *(going to Goudron)* Now, sir, this is a very bad joke!

(At this moment, we hear thunder rumbling very distinctly.)

GOUDRON: *(frightened, seizing his arm)* What's that noise?

HENRI: *(disengaging himself)* It is just the storm.

(The following five lines should overlap.)

GOUDRON: *(panic-stricken)* The storm!

MME. JOYEUSE: *(horrified, groaning)* The storm! Oh my God! *(she hides her face in her hands and goes to cower in a corner of the room, under an armchair.)*

MLLE. EUGENIE: The storm! I'm scared! *(Groaning as well, she throws herself on the ground, flat on her stomach)* Oh!

PLUME: The storm! Hide me! . . . Hide me! *(Trembling, teeth chattering, he hides under the mantlepiece, his face in the fireplace.)*

ROBERT: *(his face contorted with fear)* We're lost!

(He climbs like a cat onto the mantlepiece, his face pressed against the mirror. At this moment, blackout on stage. A streak of lightning lights up the room,

then after several seconds, a violent thunder clap sounds. All the insane start to howl. Jean and Henri remain frozen in their tracks, terrified.)

GOUDRON: *(jumping onto the desk and waving wildly amidst the lamentations)* Silence, I tell you! Silence! You're going to attract the thunder here . . . I order you to be quiet! When will you stop your moaning? What good will it do you? I am the master, do you hear? Silence!

JEAN: *(to Henri)* Let's get out of here! It's not safe here!

HENRI: *(to Jean)* Each one is crazier than the next!

JEAN: What have we gotten ourselves into?

(They cross the room rapidly, moving for the door stage right, when suddenly Goudron jumps down from the desk and blocks their way.)

GOUDRON: *(sneering)* Don't be afraid, don't be afraid . . . *(looking under the door)* Easy, now! He's come in. Don't frighten him. The door must be locked. *(He locks it and puts the key in his pocket.)* Now we have him. We have the thunder! *(He points to Jean)* Grab him! We've got him . . . help me! *(Plume, Robert and Goudron rush at Jean.)* He can no longer escape us!

JEAN: *(fighting back, stretched out on the desk where they have thrown him)* Help! Let me go!

(They struggle.)

HENRI: *(fighting against Mme. Joyeuse and Mlle. Eugenie, who have jumped on him and are scratching him as they scream.)* Will you let him go, you bastards!

GOUDRON: *(jumping on the table and indicating Jean's head)* Wait . . . Give me a knife so I can dig around in his eye . . .

(He takes the letter opener from the desk.)

PLUME: Yes, tear out his eye.

JEAN: *(still struggling on the table)* Help me! Henri . . .

PLUME: The blood is flowing. Ha, ha! *(He starts to laugh.)*

HENRI: *(still fighting off the women)* Miserable lunatics! Ahh!

ROBERT: *(pointing to the window)* Let's throw him out the window! Out the window!

GOUDRON: *(opening the window)* Yes, out the window!

(Jean, carried by Goudron, Robert, and Plume, struggles and grabs desperately onto the curtains, which begin to rip.)

JEAN: Help me!

(Henri finally frees himself from the women, who then run out to the balcony, laughing hysterically. He runs to the door stage right, tries to open it.)

HENRI: It's locked . . . *(Pounding with his fists.)* Help! Will no one come? *(Howling)* HELP!

(He comes back toward the lunatics who have taken Jean onto the balcony to throw him over. A window pane breaks in the struggle. At this moment, there is a violent knocking at the door, stage left, and several voices are heard. The following three lines should be said simultaneously:)

VOICES: *(behind the door)* Open up! Open up!

HENRI: *(who is on the balcony, trying to free Jean)* The door is locked! Break it down!

VOICES: What's going on? Robert! Plume! Goudron! Are you in there? *(they start to ram the door.)* They shouldn't all be in there . . .

HENRI: *(from the balcony)* Hurry! Help!

JEAN: We've been trapped by the lunatics. Help!

(The door gives way and several guards rush in. The insane, frightened by the voices of their guards, release Jean, and run to hide, trembling, in a corner of the room.)

SCENE VI—Goudron, Plume, Robert, Mlle. Eugenie, Mme. Joyeuse, Henri, Jean, Chief Guard, other guards

(The following five lines should be said almost together.)

CHIEF GUARD: *(entering)* What's going on?

FIRST GUARD: They're killing each other.

SECOND GUARD: *(jumping on Plume and Robert)* Here are a couple of them. Plume . . . Robert.

FIRST GUARD: *(seizing Robert)* Goudron, too.

SECOND GUARD: *(grabbing Goudron)* The most dangerous ones.

FIRST GUARD: That's not all of them.

SECOND GUARD: The others must have escaped.

CHIEF GUARD: We'll find them later. Take them away; the men to their cells, the women to the showers. And do it gently—don't bully them. What happened was our fault. That will teach us to watch them a little closer. *(The lunatics, led by the guards, exit each with a different noise: Plume laughing, Robert imitating the cork popping, and the women imitating the rooster. Then, to Henri and Jean:)* And what are you doing here? *(to Goudron, who is struggling with two guards.)* Ah! Easy, Goudron . . . or I'll put you in a straitjacket. Now be reasonable! *(noticing Goudron's medal)* Well, now you're decorated! Where did he get that? *(Goudron puts up even fiercer resistance.)* Go on take him away!

GOUDRON: *(gesticulating, now raving mad)* Silence, I tell you! Silence! I order you to be quiet! When will you stop your moaning? What good will it do you? I am the master, do you hear? I am the master!

(He throws himself on the ground, screaming, and fights against the two guards, who throw their arms around him. He bites one on the hand.)

FIRST GUARD: *(releasing Goudron and crying out in pain)* Ah! The savage! He bit me!

CHIEF GUARD: *(helping the others to get hold of him)* Goudron! You're going to spoil it . . . You don't want to keep still? You want to force me to punish you? All right, the straitjacket . . . Go on, the straitjacket!

GOUDRON: *(screaming as he is picked up by the guards)* I am the master, do you hear? I am the master!

(His cries fade out as he is carried off and away.)

Scene VII—Jean, Henri, Chief Guard

HENRI: Well! You arrived just in time! *(Indicating Jean, who has fallen into a chair, clothes torn, his face bloody.)* Get some water, quick.

CHIEF GUARD: *(taking the carafe from the mantelpiece)* Why are you here?

HENRI: *(attending to Jean, aided by the Guard)* We're reporters. We came to visit the institution . . . We found the place wide open.

CHIEF GUARD: I can believe it! The inmates had just revolted! They had us locked up in their cells. Fortunately, one of my men managed to escape and free the rest of us.

JEAN: I was almost thrown out the window!

HENRI: They could have torn out your eye . . .

CHIEF GUARD: Tell me, who received you here? Did you finally meet someone?

HENRI: The one they carried off last.

CHIEF GUARD: Goudron!

HENRI: We took him to be the director . . .

CHIEF GUARD: Well then, you got off cheap! That's the most dangerous lunatic in the institution! He was the one who organized the revolt.

JEAN: He's got quite a grip! He half strangled me.

CHIEF GUARD: Oh! When he has one of his attacks, he becomes ferocious.

(Three guards enter.)

Scene VIII—the same, the guards

FIRST GUARD: All done, Chief.

SECOND GUARD: Should we run into town and try to catch the others?

CHIEF GUARD: Oh, they can't be far. Still, warn the police. *(Just as the two guards are about to leave, he stops them)* Tell me . . . where has our director gone?

(The guards exchange looks)

FIRST GUARD: Monsieur Maillard . . .

SECOND GUARD: That's right.

THIRD GUARD: They would have locked him up like us . . .

SECOND GUARD: Unless he had the time to escape . . .

FIRST GUARD: And to go find help in town to come free us.

CHIEF GUARD: *(very anxious)* My God! So long as nothing has happened to him. Search . . . search everywhere.

(From here on, the scene must be played very quickly, until the end.)

HENRI: *(who has been listening, suddenly moves in to them)* Wait! When we entered this room there were sounds, there . . . in that room. *(He indicates the door stage left.)* I went and knocked . . . Goudron came out.

CHIEF GUARD: *(astonished)* Well!

HENRI: And while we talked with him, we heard groans . . .

CHIEF GUARD: *(pointing to the door)* That came from there?

JEAN: *(getting up)* Yes! Then he left us abruptly and went back in there, twice.

CHIEF GUARD: It's a darkroom we use for photography!

HENRI:	He came out of there all scratched and bloody!
CHIEF GUARD:	*(frightened)* Oh, my God!
HENRI:	*(looking at the stage left door, cries out suddenly)* Oh!
ALL GUARDS:	What is it?
HENRI:	*(pointing at the floor)* There . . . Look . . . Under the door!

(The guards approach)

JEAN:	*(also moving closer)* Those red spots—it's blood!

(They draw back, terror-stricken)

CHIEF GUARD:	Oh, my God! If it were . . .

(He rushes into the room stage left, followed by the guards. Long silence. Henri and Jean remain frozen with fear, eyes glued to the doorway. Then, a loud, horrified scream rings out, and the guards come out of the room, with pale faces, and their hair standing on end in horror.)

JEAN:	*(moving toward them)* Well?
HENRI:	*(approaching, as well)* What is it?
FIRST GUARD:	*(stopping them)* Don't go in there . . .
SECOND GUARD:	It's horrible!
CHIEF GUARD:	*(panic-stricken)* Go get the police . . . a doctor . . . It's monstrous, monstrous . . .

(At this moment, the third guard drags out the director's body, a horrible corpse, mutilated, gory, the face completely slashed by a razor. Everyone shrinks back from this horrifying sight and turns his head as the corpse is dragged across the stage. And we hear in the background the shrill screams of the lunatics who begin to laugh and sing again. The curtain falls slowly.)

THE END

A Drama in Two Acts
by André de Lorde and Alfred Binet
(1925)

(Translated from the French by André Gisiger)
(Adapted by Mel Gordon)

CHARACTERS:

The Sister
Madame Robin
The Normandy Woman
Hunchback
Louise
The Doctor
The Intern, Lebrun
One-Eye
Second Sister, Sister Agnes

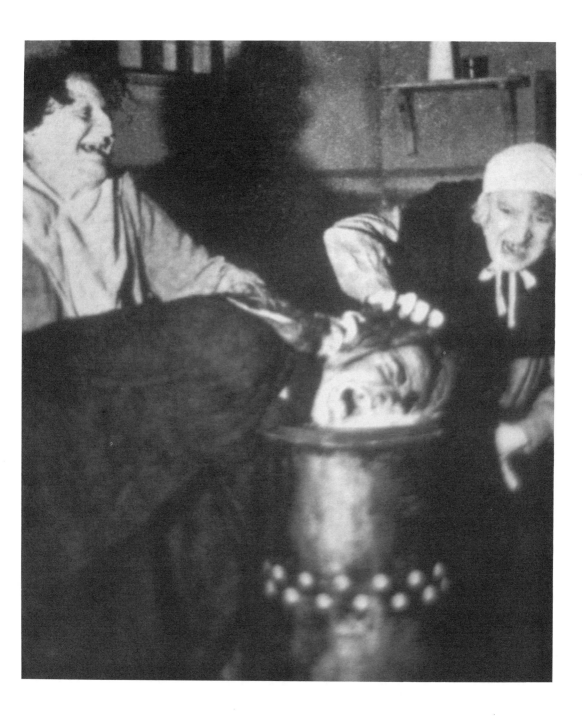

(*The play unfolds in a small room of a madhouse in Saint-Léger in Normandy. The asylum walls are whitewashed with doors on each side. A window faces the left side and a black crucifix sits on a wall shelf. There are three beds, each with a small table on the side. A cast-iron stove stands between the second and the third beds.*)

ACT I

(*When the curtain rises, the Sister, sitting in one corner, prays with her rosary. A bell chimes in the distance.*)

(*Madame Robin enters from left.*)

MADAME ROBIN: Sister!

THE SISTER: (*Finishing her prayer*) One moment!

MADAME ROBIN: (*Mysteriously*) Excuse me, Sister! Please excuse me! I didn't know you were busy.

THE SISTER: (*Puts down her rosary and makes the sign of the Cross.*) Well, what is the matter?

MADAME ROBIN: The doctor told me that he'll be here shortly with the intern.

THE SISTER: Good. Thank you. Is the dinner meal finished already?

MADAME ROBIN: No, Sister, but I wasn't very hungry tonight. I left before the others.

THE SISTER: (*Putting on her glasses*) Then pass me my knitting box. Over there, on the shelf.

MADAME ROBIN: Yes, Sister. (*Hands her the box.*) I am going to prepare the beds and evening lamp.

THE SISTER: Remember to put everything back in its place, so things aren't scattered about!

MADAME ROBIN: (*Arranges the beds.*) You don't have to tell me that. No one is more organized than me. Ever since I was given a private room, I spend most of my time putting things in order. That is my pleasure. And I have been here quite a long time. Là là!

THE SISTER: (*Walking around*) How long have you been in this asylum?

MADAME ROBIN: Forty years. (*Thinks.*) Forty years! That was the time of Doctor Delbec. He died. His intern's name was Monsieur Bernier. He died, too. And then, there was also a Sister, Sister Félicité. She died. Everybody is dead. How very funny!

(*She fixes the bed lamp and gets the evening materials from the wall shelf.*)

THE SISTER: Why do you stay here when you are cured? Have you no family?

MADAME ROBIN: Oh, yes, Sister! Just, you know, when one has been in the asylum for so long, it is difficult to get used to the outside world. Family look strangely at you. They fear that your sickness will return. When people know that you've come from the madhouse, you are treated as if you are contaminated. Therefore, one is quite happy to return to Saint-Léger. If only to die.

(*At that moment, distant cries of anguish are heard.*)

THE SISTER: What was that?

MADAME ROBIN: (*Looks through the window.*) Nothing. It's that Marie with her episodes! (*Takes back her thought.*) If I were that girl . . .

THE SISTER: What girl?

MADAME ROBIN: (*Points to the bed by the window.*) Well, the girl who sleeps there, little Louise. She has more fortune than I have had. She's young! She can still achieve happiness. Sister, when she is completely cured, can she return home?

THE SISTER: (*Disinterested*) That's what people say.

MADAME ROBIN: You know, Sister, her family are good people. I know them from the countryside.

THE SISTER: (*Contemptuously as she places the box on the table*) Puhh! They raised their daughter in strange ways.

MADAME ROBIN: Ah!

THE SISTER: She's a child who knows nothing.

MADAME ROBIN: Yet she knows how to read.

THE SISTER: She knows how to read, but she doesn't know her prayers. I even question if she believes in God!

MADAME ROBIN: Don't be angry at her, Sister. It's not her fault that her parents have raised her . . . *au naturel*.

THE SISTER: Not believing in God, you call that *au naturel*!

MADAME ROBIN: Sister, there are certain things you don't know outside of Mother Superior's teachings!

THE SISTER: Stubborn as a mule! And she already has the soul of the madwoman! Twenty times I begged her to go to the chapel. But no such luck! When she leaves here, she shall behave like a good Catholic, that little nothing! And if she doesn't . . . People without religion are merely beasts of the field!

(*A bell rings.*)

MADAME ROBIN: (*Looks through the window.*) Ah! Now it's the end of the meal. I must go. There are faces I would not like to see here.

THE SISTER: Of whom do you speak?

MADAME ROBIN: (*Pointing at the two beds*) The two dirty mad ones who sleep here: Hunchback and the Normandy Woman. What bitches!

THE SISTER: That does it! Listen, Madame Robin!

MADAME ROBIN: Excuse me, Sister. Excuse me! It slipped out. The thought was stronger than me.

THE SISTER: What do you have against them? They are two poor crazed women.

MADAME ROBIN: Two dangerous crones. Malicious madwomen.

THE SISTER: I have never noticed anything like that. With me, they are obedient and gentle.

MADAME ROBIN: In front of you, Sister. Crazy people are like everybody else. There are bad ones, mean ones, and ones who concoct evil plots. One has to be on one's guard always with them! Where do they come from, those two witches?

THE SISTER: I don't know.

MADAME ROBIN: I heard that each one went mad from grief, after losing a daughter. Is that true?

THE SISTER: Yes.

MADAME ROBIN: Well, nowadays they can't even look at a young girl without becoming envious, without having the urge to hurt her. As if they are reliving an episode!

THE SISTER: Whom do they wish to hurt?

MADAME ROBIN: (*Pointing at a bed*) Her!

THE SISTER: Little Louise?

MADAME ROBIN: Yes. While cleaning the rooms I have realized certain things. In the next room, the old woman who has just one eye, you know the one who sleeps behind the door there?

THE SISTER: Ah, yes! One-Eye!

MADAME ROBIN: You can't maintain, Sister, that she is a good Catholic! She was condemned to die for having murdered children. They have even given her a nickname: the Ogress!

THE SISTER: She is a poor demented woman. The doctors already declared her legally insane. And the courts acquitted her of any criminal responsibility!

MADAME ROBIN: In any case, accused murderers should never be incarcerated with mad people. They have to be placed in separate asylums. Otherwise, there are unfortunate possibilities!

THE SISTER: The woman has been paralyzed for six years. For six years she has not moved from her bed. There's nothing to fret about.

MADAME ROBIN: You claim!

THE SISTER: How anxious you are! Nobody's in danger here. The asylum is well guarded. There are ten Sisters alone for the women's wing.

MADAME ROBIN: Yes, during the day. But at night, the patients are alone.

THE SISTER: That is the regimen.

MADAME ROBIN: I understand. It's not your fault. You have enough work during the day so you need to rest during the night.

THE SISTER: At night we pray. We pray for you.

MADAME ROBIN: Nevertheless, there are asylums where they do nightly rounds. But not here.

THE SISTER: Nothing bad has ever happened here.

MADAME ROBIN: It needs to occur only once!

(*Shuffling can be heard from the left and right. The insane are returning to their rooms.*)

THE SISTER: Would you stay here for a moment to watch the patients, Madame Robin? I will inform Sister Placide about the Mass tonight.

MADAME ROBIN: What Mass?

THE SISTER: Sister Sulpice died this morning. The whole Order will hold a wake for the body, tonight in the chapel.

(*She exits left.*)

MADAME ROBIN: (*Alone*) Poor Sister Sulpice! She was the one good Sister.

(*From the right, the Normandy Woman and the Hunchback enter. They are two small old malicious-looking women, with diabolic expressions on their faces.*)

MADAME ROBIN: Ah, here they come there, the crones!

NORMANDY WOMAN: (*Looks around.*) Psst. She isn't here yet!

NORMANDY WOMAN: (*Looks around.*) Psst. She isn't here yet!

HUNCHBACK: (*In a low voice*) She has to pass through the courtyard.

NORMANDY WOMAN: Right. Then we have to go see One-Eye.

HUNCHBACK: She's waiting for us.

NORMANDY WOMAN: She's in charge.

HUNCHBACK: And when she screams . . .

NORMANDY WOMAN: That's the sign of death!

MADAME ROBIN: What are you mumbling about? (*The Normandy Woman laughs.*) Why are you laughing?

NORMANDY WOMAN: Are you the Bastard of Chambourcy?

HUNCHBACK: He gave a bribe to the caretaker of the cemetery. The porter told him: "It is closed from nine o'clock at night until eight o'clock in the morning. By the grave of my mother." Amen.

NORMANDY WOMAN: Amen.

(*Both of them make the sign of the Cross.*)

MADAME ROBIN: (*Lifts her shoulders and laughs.*) They are completely mad! There are times when they make you giddy even though you don't feel like it!

NORMANDY WOMAN: (*Crosses to Louise's bed and turns to Hunchback.*) Here. Look!

HUNCHBACK: The head over here.

NORMANDY WOMAN: The feet over there.

HUNCHBACK: Ha! Ha!

NORMANDY WOMAN: Ha! Ha!

MADAME ROBIN: Are you done yet? Go to sleep! That would be healthier still for the two of you. What do you have against that girl? What has she done to you?

NORMANDY WOMAN: There are some things one cannot talk about. Do you understand?

HUNCHBACK: And if one talks about them, that person is cursed!

MADAME ROBIN: Yes. That's right! So, listen: if you continue to frighten her with your gestures, to make her miserable . . . I saw the other day how you tried to trip her. I may tell the doctor about that! Perhaps he will put the restraining jacket on you again. (*To the Normandy Woman*) Like the other night!

NORMANDY WOMAN   (*Frightened*) Ah! Shut up! Shut up, stupid wench!

(*She exits left.*)

HUNCHBACK: (*Following her*) Toad! Slimy toad!

MADAME ROBIN: (*To herself*) Nothing else makes them afraid. Now where did they go? (*She looks through the open door.*) There! They went to One-Eye's bed. What could they be talking about, the three of them? They're looking at me. And what evil eyes they have! They even make me afraid, the nasty crones. (*She slams the left door as Louise enters from the right.*) I refuse to sleep in this wing!

(*Louise, an eighteen-year-old girl, pretty, with blonde hair, but timid and sickly-looking, enters.*)

LOUISE: (*Happy*) Ah! Good evening, Madame Robin. I am delighted to see you. Why are you still here?

MADAME ROBIN: I'm waiting for the Sister. She's returning soon. Good evening, my darling. How are you?

LOUISE: Fine!

MADAME ROBIN: It's fitting that you depart from here . . . that you leave soon.

LOUISE: It is over, Madame Robin! I am finally cured.

MADAME ROBIN: But are you happy?

LOUISE: Oh! Yes. There is no one I am going to miss when I leave here except for you. You were so nice to me!

MADAME ROBIN: The feeling is mutual! It was the least I could do. You are so gentle, so good-hearted! Every time you received something from the outside, you always shared it with me.

LOUISE: It's so tedious, the asylum. One has to share the little bits of pleasure.

(*She looks around.*)

MADAME ROBIN: What are you looking for?

LOUISE: They haven't returned yet?

MADAME ROBIN: Yes, they're over there, on the other side, with One-Eye.

LOUISE: Ah!

MADAME ROBIN: I don't know what they're up to. They are always conspiring.

LOUISE: Yes. Listen, Madame Robin, I need to confess to you. Those three women there, they frighten me every time I go near them. When they look at me, they stare strangely. Especially One-Eye. I get the chills. What do they want from me?

MADAME ROBIN: Nothing. They are sick people. Don't pay them any attention.

LOUISE: I try, Madame Robin. But I just don't feel safe with them!

MADAME ROBIN: If it bothers you so much, why haven't you spoken to the Sister about it?

LOUISE: She doesn't listen to me. We don't have a good "rapport."

MADAME ROBIN: Then make your good rapport with God. That's what I say. Go see the doctor. You can tell him about it. He's a fine man!

LOUISE: Yes, but I don't dare to. I have only—

MADAME ROBIN: (*Hearing noise*) Quiet! The Sister!

(*Both are silent.*)

THE SISTER: (*Entering from left, she sees Louise.*) Ah, it's you! I have been informed that the doctor has decided to release you prematurely.

LOUISE: Yes, Sister. I believe . . .

THE SISTER: He has to make a new examination.

LOUISE: Sister . . .

THE SISTER: Yesterday was Sunday. But you were not at the chapel. Why was that? (*Silence*) There is no reason now, is there? I met the Monsignor and he asked me: "Sister, in the entire asylum there is only one patient who has never taken confession. She is on your wing!" Do you think that I was pleased to hear this reprimand?

LOUISE: No, Sister.

THE SISTER: You have been very sick. Twice you nearly died.

LOUISE: That's true.

THE SISTER: Suppose your illness reoccurs and you have finally lost the power to recuperate. Then Death will surely appear, knocking at your door to take you with him, and you'll be terrified. You'll wish you had confessed. But then it will be too late, my little pagan!

LOUISE: My God!

MADAME ROBIN: (*In low voice to Louise*) Look, agree with her! You know, the Sister means well. That's her job. (*Loudly*) So, until tomorrow, good night, my little one. You're not going to be here for a very long time. Everything will go by quickly. Good night, Sister.

THE SISTER: Good night.

(*The bell for the dead rings in the distance.*)

MADAME ROBIN: (*As she exits right*) Listen how that rings! That poor Sister Sulpice!

LOUISE: (*Shuddering when hearing the bells*) Those bells! So frightening!

(*The doctor enters from left with the intern.*)

THE DOCTOR: What is the bell for the dead all about? Did somebody die?

THE SISTER: Yes, Doctor. Sister Sulpice, this morning, at eleven o'clock, during the Saint's Mass. The entire Order sat at her deathbed.

THE DOCTOR: (*Ironically*) And the sick, during that time, what happened to them? Who took care of them?

THE SISTER: We weren't absent very long!

THE DOCTOR: I hope not. And here, anything new?

THE SISTER: No, Doctor. Everything is quiet . . . as usual.

THE DOCTOR: No fever, no eruptions, no convulsions?

THE SISTER: Nothing at all.

THE DOCTOR: Okay, wonderful. (*To the intern*) Are you coming, Lebrun?

(*They prepare to leave.*)

LOUISE: Sister!

THE SISTER: What do you want?

LOUISE: I would like to talk to the doctor!

THE SISTER: The doctor has no time.

THE DOCTOR: (*Returning*) But yes, Sister, but yes. Do you have something you want to ask me, my child?

LOUISE: Yes, doctor. Oh, yes.

THE INTERN: (*Aside to the doctor*) She is pretty, that little one.

THE DOCTOR: Isn't she?

THE INTERN: With her blond hair and her pleading behavior, makes you think of Ophelia. Isn't that true, Sister?

THE SISTER: (*Disinterested*) I don't know.

THE DOCTOR: Now, my child, what is it you want from me? Sister, bring us some chairs. Here, sit down. I assume you want to discuss your leaving.

LOUISE: Yes, Doctor.

THE DOCTOR: And why do you want to leave?

LOUISE: Because I'm cured. You have cured me.

THE DOCTOR: Yes, maybe. I think you look a lot better. Your eyes look healthier, don't they?

(*He turns to the intern.*)

THE INTERN: Certainly the facial expression is more lively, more intelligent.

THE DOCTOR: You see! I diagnosed her from a depressive-manic profile according to Kraeplen. Whereas you . . .

THE INTERN: Me, I see her as more of a precocious insanity.

THE DOCTOR: If that's so, she wouldn't be in such a condition she is in today.

THE INTERN: Sometimes there are remissions.

THE DOCTOR: Not very likely.

(*The left door opens. A woman's head appears and addresses the Sister in an aside.*)

THE WOMAN: Sister, it's time for the coffin.

THE SISTER: Good. I'll be right there.

(*The Sister exits left as the death bells sound in the distance.*)

THE DOCTOR: (*To Louise*) So, you no longer suffer from your anxieties or hallucinations?

LOUISE: Me?

THE DOCTOR: You don't remember them anymore? Even better!

LOUISE: No, I'm feeling fine, Doctor. I feel—I am—how can I say it, I feel like I'm resurrected. I feel like returning to my home.

THE DOCTOR: I understand that. But one still has to be reasonable. (*To the intern*) Where is she from?

THE INTERN: From Fécamp, I believe.

LOUISE: Yes, my parents live over there.

THE DOCTOR: When it overpowered you, your crisis, you stayed with them?

LOUISE: Oh, no! I wasn't with them. I traveled. I've traveled since I was ten years old. I was adopt—

THE DOCTOR: So, your adopted family were the ones who discovered that you were mentally disturbed?

LOUISE: Yes.

THE DOCTOR: Do you think, after that, they would take you back?

LOUISE: I don't know.

THE DOCTOR: Everyone in the region will know that you have been at Saint-Léger. It's going to be quite difficult now to find another place to stay. You see, for patients released from the asylum, life can be unusually hard.

LOUISE: That's true. (*Suddenly secure*) But since I am cured, you can't keep me in the asylum for eternity! This is not a human existence.

THE DOCTOR: Of course, but wait a little bit.

LOUISE: Wait?

THE DOCTOR: Yes. Stay a little bit longer. It isn't fun, but it can only help you.

LOUISE: Oh, no!

THE DOCTOR: But yes, yes. And then, that will give us more time to observe you.

LOUISE: No. You see, I have to leave.

THE DOCTOR: Where are you going when you leave here? Do you have any idea?

LOUISE: I'll go to Paris.

THE DOCTOR: To Paris!

LOUISE: It's a big city. One always finds some work.

THE DOCTOR: Do you know anyone there?

LOUISE: No, but that doesn't matter. I will arrange it myself.

THE DOCTOR: You don't know a thing about Paris! Paris, my poor little one, pretty as you are, will swallow you up. And you'll experience so much misery, so much melancholy that your condition will return! But I will not permit that!

LOUISE: Doctor . . .

THE DOCTOR: No, no, be reasonable.

LOUISE: You don't want me to leave?

THE DOCTOR: Of course, I do, but not immediately. First of all, you will receive my personal care. (*To the intern*) Remind me. (*To Louise*) And then, when I've found a nice place for you on the outside . . .

LOUISE: When?

THE DOCTOR: When? I don't know. Maybe in fifteen days, maybe in a week.

LOUISE: (*Energetically*) I don't want to wait!

THE DOCTOR: What?

LOUISE: One more week here! No, I can't!

THE DOCTOR: Calm down, calm down!

LOUISE: I don't want to stay here anymore! I want to leave! (*Lowering her voice*) I don't want to sleep in this room anymore.

THE DOCTOR: (*Shocked by her tone*) I see, there are other things . . . other things you haven't told me! (*He notices Louise looking away.*) Why are you looking over there?

LOUISE: I was checking whether the Sister is listening.

THE DOCTOR: You have problems with her? (*Louise lowers her head, not responding.*) That doesn't surprise me. But what has she done to you—made your life miserable? Because you didn't go to Mass?

LOUISE: Yes, maybe. But that's not it!

THE DOCTOR: So what is it? You can tell us. Is it something that happened under her care?

LOUISE: Yes, in this room.

THE DOCTOR: What happened?

LOUISE: That night, no one was here . . .

THE DOCTOR: No one? What about the other patients?

LOUISE: Yes, but the Sisters were gone. And then . . .

THE DOCTOR: Yes? Stop trembling. (*He takes her hand in a fatherly manner.*) Tell us.

LOUISE: I don't know how to say it. Just thinking about it turns my stomach!

THE DOCTOR: Please, calm down.

LOUISE: Fine. When the Sisters leave, when the lights are out, if you only knew how everything changes in the wing.

THE DOCTOR: What changes?

LOUISE: There are things going on that you don't understand. First, there is that door over there, you see!

(*She points to the left door.*)

THE DOCTOR: Yes?

LOUISE: The Sister locks it when she departs. Last night, in the early morning, the door opened.

THE DOCTOR:　You saw someone open that door?

LOUISE:　It opened by itself. It was like a signal. The two old ones who sleep there, do you know them?

THE DOCTOR:　Yes. Continue.

LOUISE:　They got up.

THE DOCTOR:　What? They got up?

LOUISE:　Since there was no one there to stop them.

THE DOCTOR:　Excuse me, but one of the women, the one from Normandy, wore a restraining jacket that I personally tied her in that night.

LOUISE:　What does that do? The other one pulled her out of it.

THE DOCTOR:　It requires a key.

LOUISE:　She *has* a key. She has everything it takes to—

(*She stops.*)

THE DOCTOR:　To what?

LOUISE:　I see how you stare at me! The both of you!

THE DOCTOR:　(*To his intern*) I fear she still can't take any agitation.

THE INTERN:　Obviously not.

LOUISE:　My God! Do you think that I am lying or still mad?

THE DOCTOR:　No, my child. So, from the beginning, what did they do?

LOUISE:　Without a sound they crept close to my bed. They leaned over me, they watched me . . . with a fixed stare like they wanted to hurt me.

THE INTERN:　To hurt her!

LOUISE:　But they didn't dare. They looked towards the door and they shook their heads: "No, no . . ." as if they were afraid. It seemed as if they spoke to someone else. And there *was* somebody else.

THE DOCTOR: Who was it?

LOUISE: One-Eye, who gestured to them.

THE DOCTOR: You think so?

LOUISE: Oh! I recognized her immediately with the black patch over her eye. She made signs.

THE DOCTOR: It's impossible.

LOUISE: Doctor, I saw her.

THE DOCTOR: I tell you, it is impossible! True, the other two women are not crippled. But the so-called One-Eye has been paralyzed in both legs for six years. She is bedridden. Therefore, she cannot rise or stand.

LOUISE: But I did see her, Doctor. She was there in front of the door, standing!

THE DOCTOR: I see, my child, that you are not yet cured!

LOUISE: I am cured. My mind is healed.

THE DOCTOR: No, since you claim things that are impossible—

LOUISE: I don't know how to convince you, but I did see her. I wasn't asleep. My eyes were wide open. I did see her. The signs she made to the others. They were in fear. I absolutely saw her!

THE INTERN: (*To the doctor*) She is having hallucinations again.

THE DOCTOR: That's what I think, too.

THE INTERN: It is quite possible, what she is telling us—

THE DOCTOR: (*Interrupting*)—are the warnings of a new crisis. Poor little one!

LOUISE: (*Frightened*) No, Doctor. (*To the intern*) But no, Monsieur, I tell you, I did see her.

THE DOCTOR: Of course, you saw it. You think you saw it. (*In an aside to the intern*) Now I've made up my mind.

THE INTERN: Me, too.

THE DOCTOR: The hallucinations have returned.

LOUISE: No, Doctor. No! I'm not mad anymore! Doctor, you can see that I'm in my right mind at this moment!

THE DOCTOR: Calm down!

LOUISE: I am excited but not crazy. I am not telling you stories. (*To the intern*) Isn't that true, Monsieur? I don't tell stories. Please believe me, I beg of you!

THE DOCTOR: (*To placate her*) Certainly, I believe you! I just need to make a few additional observations over the next couple of days.

LOUISE: For a few more days? And if it happens again at night?

THE DOCTOR: You'll inform me.

LOUISE: But you're not going to leave me here? If I can't leave immediately, at least put me in a different wing!

THE DOCTOR: All the beds are taken at the moment.

LOUISE: I beg of you!

THE DOCTOR: Then tomorrow you will change wings. I promise you.

LOUISE: Yes, but tonight . . . I'm so frightened! So frightened!

THE INTERN: What a state she puts herself in!

THE DOCTOR: Tonight the Sister is not going to leave you.

LOUISE: She will leave!

THE DOCTOR: I am going to give her an order.

LOUISE: She will leave!

THE DOCTOR: I'd like to see her try!

LOUISE: She will go as soon you have left!

THE DOCTOR: (*Harshly*) That's enough! If you continue to be so obstinate, that alone proves that you're not cured and I will be forced to keep you in the asylum . . . for a substantial period.

LOUISE: My God!

(*The Sister enters from left.*)

THE DOCTOR: (*Calling her*) Sister!

THE SISTER: Doctor . . .

THE DOCTOR: I came to scold this child because of her unreasonable nature. She is still very nervous. She is constantly afraid without reason. But, nevertheless, she suffers, and we must spare her of any unnecessary suffering. Tonight you will watch over her.

THE SISTER: But, Doctor . . .

THE DOCTOR: Please! Your presence will prevent her nightmares.

THE SISTER: Nightmares are immaterial!

THE DOCTOR: They're important enough to be cared for.

THE SISTER: If she becomes too agitated, we could give her two spoonfuls of chloral.

THE DOCTOR: No, I prefer that you stay with her.

THE SISTER: That will be difficult for me, especially tonight.

THE DOCTOR: Why is that?

THE SISTER: We have a service.

THE DOCTOR: What service?

THE SISTER: For Sister Sulpice.

THE DOCTOR: Ah, yes!

THE SISTER: There will be a wake all night long to sing hymns, and all the Sisters are assisting.

THE DOCTOR: You will have to find someone to replace you.

THE SISTER: (*Bluntly*) That is impossible.

THE DOCTOR: That is *very* possible, if you want it.

THE SISTER: The Abbess will not tolerate anyone's absence for this service.

THE DOCTOR: I have to remind you that there are matters of humanity that are more important than the service in the chapel.

THE SISTER: I don't think so. It depends on one's point of view.

THE DOCTOR: I'm surprised that you hesitate, when I insist that your duty is to remain here.

THE SISTER: My duty is to obey the Mother Superior.

THE DOCTOR: Watching over the dead is good, but there are certain things of greater importance, which is to treat the living.

THE SISTER: (*Stubbornly*) My duty is to obey the Mother Superior.

THE DOCTOR: You must obey me first of all. The Mother Superior is not in charge of the halls of this asylum. It is me, the Medical Doctor! Do you understand that?

THE SISTER: (*Blankly*) Yes, Doctor.

THE DOCTOR: I insist that you stay the night, the *whole* night, in *this* room. Are you going to obey or not?

THE SISTER: I am nothing but a servant. My duty is to obey.

(*She mumbles some words.*)

THE DOCTOR: What did you say?

THE SISTER: Nothing, Doctor. I said nothing. I am permitted to say nothing.

THE DOCTOR: (*Sternly*) That's good. (*To Louise affectionately*) I hope you're finally assured. (*Louise doesn't respond.*) Good evening, my child. Good night. (*To the intern*) Ah, the Sisters! The Sisters! (*As he departs*) They have great qualities. They don't make any noise. They are serious, devoted. But when it comes to ceremony they are stubborn!

(*The doctor and intern exit right, followed by the Sister.*)

LOUISE: (*Alone, she sits down on her bed.*) They didn't want to believe me. (*Lamenting*) My God! My God! (*The Normandy Woman and Hunchback reenter from the left. In the dark, they slowly advance toward Louise, who becomes frightened again and lets out a shriek.*) Ah!

NORMANDY WOMAN: You shouldn't be afraid like that, my little darling.

HUNCHBACK: We haven't even touched you yet and you scream.

NORMANDY WOMAN: Wait a little.

HUNCHBACK: A little bit.

NORMANDY WOMAN: The night is long!

HUNCHBACK: Yes, the night. It is good, the night.

LOUISE: Why do you look at me like that?

NORMANDY WOMAN: Can't we look at you?

HUNCHBACK: You are pretty.

NORMANDY WOMAN: Your eyes especially.

HUNCHBACK: They are not yours.

NORMANDY WOMAN: Certainly not.

HUNCHBACK: The old hag said it, "There's a cuckoo inside."

NORMANDY WOMAN: And, one day, she will fly away.

HUNCHBACK: (*Making flapping movements*) Pfftt! Pfftt!

LOUISE: Go away. Don't come any closer. (*Calling*) Sister!

NORMANDY WOMAN: Don't be frightened, little one, the cuckoo will be released soon!

(*They laugh as they move closer to Louise.*)

(*The Sister reappears through the right door while the two old crones silently climb in their beds.*)

THE SISTER: What is it? Who called for me? You, again?

LOUISE: (*Emotionally*) Yes, Sister.

THE SISTER: It's always the complainers who waste our time. What is it now?

LOUISE: (*Pointing at the two women*) They're here.

THE SISTER: Of course, they are here, because they sleep in the same room as you do. So go to bed now, all three of you. (*She strikes a match and lights the bed lamp. The room brightens. She looks around. Voices and words from the next room can be heard.*) Hey, over there! (*She takes the bed lamp, opens the left door, and looks into the room.*) Silence! No more noise! It's time to sleep. Do you hear me? (*The noise slowly dissipates into a deep silence. She locks the door with her key. The two old women prepare to sleep. Louise sits on her bed quietly. The Sister puts the lamp on the shelf. Then she kneels down at the crucifix and says a prayer in a low voice.*)

(*Hunchback and the Normandy Woman murmur a prayer—a few words can be heard: "Saint Mary . . . in the hour of our death . . . so be it!"*)

THE SISTER: Amen. (*She rises. At this moment a bell rings in the distance. The Sister listens, hesitates, and walks slowly to Louise's bed, who still hasn't moved. In a soft voice*) Louise?

LOUISE: Sister?

THE SISTER: Are you going to bed, my child?

LOUISE: (*Hesitating*) Of course, Sister.

THE SISTER: You're not afraid anymore, I hope? You see, everything is calm. You are going to have a good night, aren't you?

LOUISE: Yes, Sister.

(*The ringing begins again.*)

THE SISTER: Do you hear that bell calling me? It demands that I go and perform my duty to the dead.

LOUISE: But Sister . . .

THE SISTER: You do understand that I cannot stay here. You're not a selfish person. You have a great generosity of spirit. You know the dead need our prayers. The dead should come before the living.

LOUISE: But the Doctor—

THE SISTER: The Doctor is never going to know if you don't tell him. If you tell him, you'll cause me a lot of trouble. And then, my girl, think of all the scandal that you would cause! He makes a big thing out of everything. He'll complain to the administration and will demand an inquiry. The Abbess doesn't like that. Not at all. And we should not do anything to displease her. In fact, it's she who gives orders here. Do you understand me?

LOUISE: (*Resigned*) Yes, Sister.

THE SISTER: Good, my child. Be reasonable. We'll remain good friends, the two of us. It is in your interest, believe me. I can be helpful for your departure. So be reasonable. Good night!

(*She moves to the right door while the curtain falls slowly and the bell continues to ring in the distance.*)

ACT II

(*The same set as the first act. Through the window moonlight shines with a greenish glow while the flame of the night lamp flickers in the glass on the wall shelf. Deep silence. A clock in the distance strikes ten. During the whole act one can hear—from time to time—the sound of an organ and the psalms of prayers from the chapel. Suddenly, on their beds, Hunchback and the Normandy Woman turn silently.*)

NORMANDY WOMAN: (*In a deep voice, breaking the silence*) Psst!

HUNCHBACK: (*Replying in the same manner*) What?

NORMANDY WOMAN: (*Sitting up on her bed*) Is she asleep?

HUNCHBACK: (*Same manner*) I think so.

NORMANDY WOMAN: Make sure!

HUNCHBACK: I'll check.

NORMANDY WOMAN: Wait! Somebody is walking, somebody is talking in the hallway.

HUNCHBACK: Maybe the Sister is returning?

NORMANDY WOMAN: Maybe. (*They return to bed. Silence again; the noise grows distant. They sit up.*) They didn't come in here!

HUNCHBACK: No, they went down the stairs.

NORMANDY WOMAN: That's right.

(*Pause*)

HUNCHBACK: So, that's it for tonight.

NORMANDY WOMAN: That's what she wants.

HUNCHBACK: Must obey her. Absolutely!

NORMANDY WOMAN: Or she'll hurt us.

HUNCHBACK: Like the little one.

NORMANDY WOMAN: Remember what she demanded?

HUNCHBACK: What do you mean?

NORMANDY WOMAN: A towel.

HUNCHBACK: I don't have one.

NORMANDY WOMAN: Tear a piece out from your sheet, with your teeth!

HUNCHBACK: Good idea.

(The sound of ripping cloth can be heard.)

LOUISE: *(After dozing, she sits up.)* What?

HUNCHBACK: She's waking up.

NORMANDY WOMAN: Quiet.

(They remain still for some time.)

LOUISE: I heard. Certainly, it's here.

(She looks around the room.)

HUNCHBACK: *(Hides the piece of cloth under her pillow.)* That's it.

NORMANDY WOMAN: Wait for the signal.

HUNCHBACK: Wait.

(Silence)

LOUISE: Who is talking over there? It's them. They aren't sleeping!

(She leans forward in order to hear better.)

HUNCHBACK: There, she woke up!

NORMANDY WOMAN: She can hear us.

(They sit on their beds.)

LOUISE: What are they doing, sitting so still? (*Loudly*) What is it? What do you want?

NORMANDY WOMAN: Don't be afraid, my little darling.

HUNCHBACK: Of course.

NORMANDY WOMAN: Was it the cry of the cuckoo which woke you?

HUNCHBACK: That's a sign of death.

(*They laugh.*)

LOUISE: Be quiet! It's horrible to be here, with the mad—

NORMANDY WOMAN: Then you are even madder, you there!

HUNCHBACK: (*Laughing*) She thinks she isn't crazy anymore!

NORMANDY WOMAN: Because she will soon leave the madhouse!

HUNCHBACK: You will never leave.

NORMANDY WOMAN: If you leave, it's with your feet first!

(*They laugh.*)

LOUISE: (*Frightened*) I can't stay here anymore! Alone . . .

NORMANDY WOMAN: You are not alone!

HUNCHBACK: Because you're with us!

(*They climb off their beds.*)

LOUISE: Leave me, or I'll call . . .

(*A wheezing is heard from the room at the left. Louise, scared sick, stops. The two old crones, frightened, stay still.*)

NORMANDY WOMAN: Be quiet! It's her!

HUNCHBACK: Shut up! She enters!

NORMANDY WOMAN: If she hears us, she'll be in a rage!

HUNCHBACK: And if she is in a rage, protect yourself!

NORMANDY WOMAN: Yes, must protect myself!

HUNCHBACK: (*Praying*) "Miserere . . ."

NORMANDY WOMAN: "Miserere nobis . . ."

HUNCHBACK: When you leave . . .

NORMANDY WOMAN: . . . with your feet first . . .

HUNCHBACK: (*Pointing to the left door*) She enters! There!

LOUISE: (*In front of the window*) The door is opening by itself! Help me! Help me!

(*She attempts to run toward the right door, but the two crones block her and push her away. Panic-stricken, like an animal in a trap, Louise turns away. Suddenly, a dark figure surges up in front of her. One-Eye enters through the left door. She closes the door silently, rushes toward Louise, and knocks her down on a bed. A muffled scream is heard.*)

(*One-Eye holds Louise, who struggles on the bed as Hunchback brings the bed lamp closer.*)

ONE-EYE: Light!

HUNCHBACK: Here!

ONE-EYE: More light!

(*She puts a hand over Louise's mouth to silent her.*)

HUNCHBACK: (*With the bed lamp*) Voilà!

(*Both Hunchback and the Normandy Woman lean over Louise.*)

NORMANDY WOMAN: (*To Hunchback*) She holds her so firmly.

HUNCHBACK: She does!

NORMANDY WOMAN: What is she going to do?

HUNCHBACK: I don't know . . . but *she* knows!

ONE-EYE: Normand, do you have the cloth?

NORMANDY WOMAN: Here it is.

(*She hands her the torn-up piece of sheet.*)

ONE-EYE: (*To Normandy Woman*) Hold her hands! And give me a long needle!

HUNCHBACK: (*Searching*) A needle?

NORMANDY WOMAN: The Sister's knitting needle! On the shelf!

HUNCHBACK: (*Turning*) Ah, on the shelf.

NORMANDY WOMAN: In front of the Blessed Virgin.

HUNCHBACK: There it is!

(*She gives the knitting needle to One-Eye.*)

ONE-EYE: I can't see well enough to do my work!

(*She jams the needle in the deep pocket of her asylum gown.*)

NORMANDY WOMAN: I agree. It's too dark in here.

ONE-EYE: Bring the bed light closer!

HUNCHBACK: Here.

ONE-EYE: Closer!

(*Hunchback obeys.*)

NORMANDY WOMAN: (*Staring at Louise*) People say she's already dead. Yes, she is like a corpse.

ONE-EYE: No. When I am finished, the cuckoo will return to us!

LOUISE: (*Struggling against One-Eye's grip*) Ah!

ONE-EYE: (*Uncovering Louise's mouth*) Do you know who I am, child?

LOUISE: Where am I?

ONE-EYE: Stop moving!

LOUISE: (*Catching a glimpse of them*) What are you doing to me?

ONE-EYE: Don't scream. We don't want to do anything to you ... only to those two eyes.

LOUISE: My eyes!

ONE-EYE: Those are not your eyes!

NORMANDY WOMAN: She thinks those are her eyes.

HUNCHBACK: Ha! Ha!

NORMANDY WOMAN: Ha! Ha!

ONE-EYE: (*With authority*) Quiet, you two! Do you understand, my little one, it's a service I want to render you. You were crazy once, weren't you? Don't you remember?

NORMANDY WOMAN: Of course she does!

HUNCHBACK: She doesn't remember!

ONE-EYE: While you were crazy, a beast got inside you, a cuckoo bird. She hid in your head. Behind your eyes!

LOUISE: (*Struggling*) Ah!

ONE-EYE: If you continue to scream, I am going to have to shut you up good. So listen to me! I'm going to rid you of the bird. Do you understand? She has stolen your eyes. That bird has removed your eyeballs and put hers in your sockets! Do you understand now? (*Screaming*) Those damned cuckoo's eyes are planning to rob me of my sight!

LOUISE: (*Filled with terror*) No, no! Have pity! Please!

ONE-EYE: (*Calmly*) Now you understand.

LOUISE: I beg of you!

ONE-EYE: It'll be good for you!

LOUISE: Please! I don't want to die!

ONE-EYE: You won't die!

LOUISE: (*Struggling*) Help! Help me!

ONE-EYE: (*Her hand over Louise's mouth*) Shut up! (*To the women*) Hurry, before the screams begin!

(*One-Eye gags her with the piece of cloth, which also covers her entire face.*)

LOUISE: (*Resisting*) Ah!

ONE-EYE: Don't move, little one! It will be over soon. I only have to feel exactly . . . where your eyes are. (*Pause*) But this cloth is too stiff! It's been starched!

NORMANDY WOMAN: What?

ONE-EYE: Too much starch in the cloth, idiot! Soak the damn thing in water and dry it on the stove! I must know precisely where her eyes are, Normand!

(*One-Eye grabs the cloth from Louise's face and flings it at the Normandy Woman. One-Eye again silences Louise with her hand. Now in a panic, the Normandy Woman repeatedly dips the cloth in a water basin and throws it on the stove, which sends up plumes of steam.)*

ONE-EYE: Why did you give me a starched cloth?

NORMANDY WOMAN: It's soft now! Look, it is completely soft!

(*The Normandy Woman spreads the steaming cloth over Louise's face.)*

LOUISE: (*Screaming*) Ah!

(*One-Eye clinically touches Louise's covered face and smiles. With her other hand she pulls the knitting needle from her pocket and quickly rams it through the cloth into Louise's eye-socket.*)

LOUISE: (*A new intense screaming*) NO!!!!

ONE-EYE: There! That's it! Blood is flowing on my hands. It's warm, it's good! It's just like the blood of an infant! A tiny, beautiful child!

(*One-Eye stabs Louise's other eye.*)

LOUISE: Ah!

ONE-EYE: Like the old times!

(*One-Eye laughs hysterically and makes flapping gestures as she dances around Louise's tortured body.*)

(*In a reflexive motion the blinded Louise pulls the knitting needle from her second destroyed eye and leaps up from the bed, as the bloody cloth falls to the ground. Vitreous fluid flows down Louise's mutilated face, which is frozen in a silent scream.*)

NORMANDY WOMAN: (*Confused as she runs toward Louise*) The bird? Where's the bird?

ONE-EYE: Ha! Ha! Ha! Ha!

(*Louise instinctively ignores the Normandy Woman, lunges toward the laughing One-Eye, and falls dead, holding the needle*)

NORMANDY WOMAN: (*Inspecting the corpse of Louise*) The cuckoo didn't fly out! Hunchback, did you see the bird?

(*The crones stare at each other in disbelief as One-Eye continues her demented dance. Realizing that they had been tricked, Hunchback suddenly overpowers the ecstatic One-Eye and drags the uncomprehending ogress across the room to the stove. Hunchback forces the unseeing side of One-Eye's face down onto the red-hot plate. The face sizzles away in a burst of bloody steam as One-Eye screams wildly. Alarmed by the piercing shrieks, Hunchback lifts up the ogress' oozing head by her hair and smashes her one eye against the stove plate, killing her.*)

(*Long pause. Hunchback looks at the Normandy Woman.*)

NORMANDY WOMAN: (*Coming out of her shock*) There never was a cuckoo!

(*Noise from the right is heard.*)

HUNCHBACK: Normand, listen! Footsteps!

(*Hunchback blows out the bed lamp and climbs into her bed. The room is bathed in moonlight.*)

NORMANDY WOMAN: (*Realizing their predicament*) They're coming! They're coming!

(*She scrambles into bed and pulls a sheet over her head. A pause. Steps can be heard.*)

THE SISTER: (*Off-stage*) I assure you, Sister Agnes, I did hear noises. (*Enters, holding a lantern.*) What is it? Did someone cry out?

(*She stops at the threshold. Silence*)

SECOND SISTER: (*Entering*) No. Just as I said.

THE SISTER: (*Illuminating only the sleeping forms of the Normandy Woman and Hunchback*) Asleep. Everything is quiet.

SECOND SISTER: I told you! It's nothing at all. And you know Mother Superior doesn't like it when we leave before the end of the service.

(*A lyrical Vespers' chant of female voices can be heard in the distance.*)

THE SISTER: (*While leaving*) Yes, I was mistaken. Let's return for Communion!

(*The Sisters exit with the lantern. After the door is shut, the curtain falls slowly on the Normandy Woman and Hunchback as they rise up in their beds and begin to cackle in the moonlight.*)